Confessions of a Maverick

CONFESSIONS OF A MAVERICK

AN AUTOBIOGRAPHY

Farrington R. Carpenter

Edited and with a foreword by Marshall Sprague
Published by the State Historical Society of Colorado

Confessions of a Maverick has been generously supported
by the Farrington Carpenter family, the Carl A. Norgren
Foundation, Mr. and Mrs. Henry W. Gossard, Jr.,
Mr. Tom Lasater, Mr. and Mrs. John A. Love,
Mr. and Mrs. Robert M. Perry, and
Mr. and Mrs. Kennard P. Perry.

Portions of chapters 5 and 9 have been reprinted
by permission of *The Colorado Lawyer,* published
by the Colorado Bar Association.

Second printing, 1998

CONTENTS

Foreword by the Editor

The state of Colorado has had its fair share of strange and wonderful people but none of them matched Farrington Reed Carpenter in the length and depth of his Colorado experience. Ferry died, aged ninety-four, on December 12, 1980, at his rambling ranch home near Hayden, Colorado, on the beautiful Yampa River, near where he proved up a 160-acre homestead in 1907 while a sophomore at Princeton University.

Through his long and turbulent career, Ferry's idea of heaven on earth was northwestern Colorado. In serene isolation beyond the towering Continental Divide, he gathered ideas which he used to expose the follies of life, though his was kindly scorn softened by laughter at himself and the world in general. Ferry made it a rule never to do anything the way he was expected to do it. And having done it in his own novel way, he was impatient to get along with something new.

On the frontier in New Mexico at fourteen, he learned the cowboy's skills and passed up a high school diploma. But this did not deter him from obtaining a diploma from Princeton and Harvard Law School, class of 1912. He then turned his back on the East for good and set up his law office in a Hayden bowling alley. He had a hand in bringing to Hayden its Union High School, first hospital, waterworks, sewage system, and Boy Scout troop. In 1909 he began his lifelong career of raising Hereford cattle. By 1930 he owned the largest registered Hereford herd on Colorado's Western Slope.

Ferry served for eight years as Routt County attorney and four years as district attorney for Routt, Moffat, and Grand counties, comprising an area larger than the state of Massachusetts. As an attorney, he prosecuted cattle rustlers, kidnappers, and a lady accused of murdering her husband with arsenic. He led Hayden's citizens in their war against the cricket invasion of 1927–28. He negotiated a cease-fire between hundreds of armed sheepmen and cattlemen lined up for battle south of Craig, Colorado.

As an obscure country lawyer, he challenged the state's most powerful banking syndicate, which was pleading tax leniency for the Denver and Rio Grande Railroad in what he called the "Moffat Tunnel Steal." He lost his case by a hair, but he scared the Denver syndicate so badly that *The Denver Post* nicknamed him admiringly "Dynamite Carpenter."

Along the way he sharpened his skill as a superb teller of tall tales, many of which became folklore in Routt County. In his collisions with the high and mighty, Ferry came to be called a maverick by those who tried and failed to put their brand on him and lure him into the fold of predictable people. Among those attempting to do so was Harold L. Ickes, secretary of the interior and self-styled "curmudgeon" in the administration of Franklin D. Roosevelt.

In 1934 the president named Carpenter as director of the Division of Grazing under the Taylor Grazing Act. This historic measure charged Carpenter with the responsibility of bringing federal control to 8 million acres of unclaimed public domain (soon extended to 142 million acres). But Ferry's maverick ways were too much for Secretary Ickes, who fired his grazing director three times. President Roosevelt, who admired mavericks, reinstated Ferry after every firing. In the end, Ferry resigned of his own free will, extracting from the curmudgeon a gracious letter praising his four stormy years as grazing director. In 1946 Ferry's Grazing Service and the General Land Office were merged into the Bureau of Land Management, which functions today substantially the same as did Ferry's original plan for the Taylor Grazing Act.

Addressing the Colorado Municipal League at Craig in 1970, the maverick said with some relish: "I never held a job that I didn't get fired from. I was dropped as Colorado's first director of revenue for dismissing a pack of unneeded political job-holders.

The trustees of the University of Denver fired me as their director of development because I moved too far too fast. My demands for fiscal responsibility put me out of the Colorado legislature after I had served for only one term. I was held in abomination for several years by the hierarchy of the American Hereford Association because I saw no merit in breeding cattle—as cowmen put it—for show on the hoof instead of for meat on the hook."

Though Carpenter liked to behave as a dyed-in-the-wool westerner, wearing loud shirts, galluses, string ties, cowboy boots, and a Stetson, he remained in his secret heart a man without regional ties. He was, in part, an easterner, proud of his New England–Illinois–Ivy League background.

Farrington Reed Carpenter did not allow his high ambitions to twist him out of shape. His successes had less to do with a hunger for power and wealth than with simple enjoyment in using his talents and energy to make his part of the world—Hayden and northwestern Colorado—a better place for those who lived there.

Marshall Sprague
October 1, 1981

Farrington R. Carpenter
August 10, 1886–December 12, 1980

ONE

Growing Up

A number of fine women have played important roles in my life, starting with my birth on August 10, 1886, in Evanston, Illinois, a citadel of Methodist orthodoxy on Lake Michigan north of Chicago. The date also happened to be the birthday of my father's mother, a forthright lady whose maiden name was Martha Farrington. During the excitement of my arrival, she appeared at our home at 1314 Hinman Avenue and told my mother, who had done the work of having me, and my father, who had cooperated also, that my first name was to be Farrington. I was not in a position to oppose her choice. It was too long a name for everyday use and was soon shortened to Ferry. When one of my Princeton classmates later said that Farrington sounded to him like the name of an English resort town, I avoided using it whenever I could.

My grandfather, A. B. Carpenter, a physician in Barre, Vermont, died at forty-six, leaving my father, aged twelve, as his only child. My grandmother, Martha Farrington Carpenter, married a widower, Orvis French, a carpenter with five young children. In the 1850s the combined families moved to Evanston, a village on Lake Michigan that had grown up around Northwestern University. Orvis French built a large home there which was used during the Chicago fire of 1871 by refugees fleeing to the north shore of the lake. My father used to tell me that Grandmother Martha was a "do-it" type with an "executive nose." She enlarged the French home into what became known as the French House, one of the largest and most successful boardinghouses in town.

Evanston was near the south end of lake Michigan, where it enjoyed water communication with the Atlantic Ocean through the Sault Ste Marie Canal. By reversing the flow of the Chicago River, Evanston and Chicago became connected with the Mississippi and the Gulf of Mexico. As I grew up I learned that Evanston had been named for John Evans, the founder of Northwestern University and in 1862 the second territorial governor of Colorado. Much later I met various Evans progeny in Denver and, as an upstart lawyer from a small Western Slope town called Hayden, conducted a lawsuit involving the famous Moffat Railroad Tunnel, which John Evans's son, William Gray Evans, built in 1928.

Both of my parents were New Englanders of Scotch and English descent. My mother, Marybelle Reed, was the daughter of a Massachusetts farm boy, Asa D. Reed, who had a livery stable in Boston and went west to make a fortune floating logs down the Mississippi. He moved to Illinois in 1833 after his marriage to a Connecticut girl, Eunice Clarinda Chapman. The Reeds moved to Evanston in 1861, where Asa organized and headed the City National Bank in Chicago. The Reeds' youngest daughter, my mother Marybelle, was born in 1860. She was a frail child and never attended school. She was engaged to be married to Edward Farrington Carpenter at sixteen and married him in Evanston at nineteen years of age. I was the middle of her six children—three girls and three boys—five of whom survived. She lived to be ninety-nine years and seven months of age, preserving most of her faculties until her death.

Marybelle was beautiful in her teens. Later, at 5 feet 7½ inches tall, she was the same height as Janet Patie, the famous soprano and English beauty. Her father's favorite, my mother always played backgammon with him when he came home from work. Her emotions were easily aroused, and she often said that if she had lived in India, where they hired people to cry at funerals, she was sure that she would have been kept busy. She lost her first child, a girl baby who was to be named Martha. She told me that for months thereafter she could not pass a carriage with a baby in it without being reduced to tears.

The memory of my mother's tender care of all her children stayed with me all my life. When I was very young I had a severe case of typhoid fever. I would let nobody but my mother hold me, and she did so for long hours. She always put me to bed, and after tucking me in, she would sit on the edge of the bed and talk to me. She never overlooked an opportunity to impress me with the fact that I was expected to live my life in a way that would make this world a better place to be than before my advent. Her favorite injunction was from Ecclesiastes: "Cast thy bread upon the waters: for thou shalt find it after many days."

As I grew older she explained the facts of life. At the time I rather resented the familiarity and thought that it would be more manly if I got that information back of the barn from older boys who constantly discussed such matters. Whenever mother took a tub bath, she never locked the bathroom door and encouraged her children to come in and out as our needs might demand. In that way she forestalled some of the curiosity about the human body which is left to conjecture in many families. When I reached the age of puberty, she kept track of my activities and once warned me not to play with our minister's youngest daughter, who was a subject of local gossip.

Mother's brother, Arthur Reed, had died from consumption in 1878, and she was always on the lookout for indications of the disease in her children. For fear of it one winter in the 1890s, she took the family to the health resort of Colorado Springs and put the children in school there. When my father came out to bring us back to Evanston, we all went sightseeing at the Cave of the Winds, near Manitou. Our picture was taken mounted on burros. They were rather moth-eaten little animals, but I suspect that my lifelong love of riding horseback above all other forms of transportation began then.

My father, Edward Farrington Carpenter, had the misfortune as a small boy of putting out one of his eyes when a knife slipped which he was using to make a harness for his dog. His adjustment to the wearing of a glass eye increased his determination to succeed. He never went to college, but started work at eighteen as a shoe salesman in Chicago. Later he built a shoe factory in Holland, Michigan, and served for years on the board of the National Shoe Manufacturers Association, receiving as a reward a gold watch with chimes. He was a stalwart backer of the Republican party and a pioneer member of the First Congregational Church in Evanston.

In my early years, Father spent much of his time away from home on shoe business. He handled all disciplinary problems and administered all punishment by spanking. Like his mother, Martha Farrington French, he was a "do-it" person who believed in instant action whenever a good idea occurred to him. He often said to me, "When you want something done, do it now, and don't rely on others to get it done."

My father believed in boys having chores to do, and he paid a small allowance for their performance. He reminded all of us that when he died his worldly goods would go to our mother and the girls in the family. He would give us boys as much education as we would pursue, but after that we would have to make it on our own or go to the poorhouse.

My earlier burro riding in Colorado Springs did not inspire in me much longing for western life. But my father had two cousins from Vermont, Charles and John Mead, who had gone into the cattle business in North Dakota. They had prospered, and when they shipped cattle to the Chicago stockyards to sell, they would come to Evanston to see us. They wore big black hats and had buffalo robe overcoats that hung to their ankles. I was fascinated with their stories and begged them to take me west with them. They said that there were too many Indians in North Dakota just looking for a chance to scalp young boys of my age. That remark, of course, just increased my desire to go west. At the same time, Buffalo Bill's Wild West show came to Chicago, and Mother took the family to see it. For weeks afterwards, I reenacted the memory of Buffalo Bill in his U. S. mail coach, drawn by four plunging horses and chased by screaming Indians with bows and arrows. Buffalo Bill was rescued by brave U. S. calvarymen shooting from the hip, and his show made the West seem the most thrilling place on the planet.

A neighborhood boy named Jack White was in my eighth-grade class and played with me at being Buffalo Bill. Jack had developed lung trouble and had been sent out to a ranch near Dodge City, Kansas, to recuperate. When father heard that Jack was working for his board and room on the ranch, he said to me, "Any boy of twelve years who earns his own board and room is bound to become a success in the business world." Since I had turned twelve myself, his comment made a big impression on me.

But for the moment I was preoccupied with my eighth-grade graduation from the school which we all attended across the street from our house. For reasons that I cannot explain, I let myself in for the awful chore of speaking in the graduation declamation contest. (In later years a psychologist told me that my tendency as an adult to get up before a bunch of people and talk my head off showed itself first at that graduation ceremony.)

For my recitation I chose Tennyson's "The Revenge," which told of how Sir Richard Grenville and his little ship *Revenge* was attacked by fifty-three Spanish galleons. I was approaching puberty, barely five feet tall, and dressed appropriately in wing collar and high-button shoes. My parents were present in the front row with my older sister Ruth and my brothers Kenneth and Willis. I warmed up well to Tennyson's tale and raised my fist dramatically when Sir Richard shouted, "Fight on! Fight on!" At that moment my voice cracked and some people in the audience giggled. For a full minute I froze, until my teacher prompted me in a loud whisper, "And the night went down, and the sun smiled." Somehow I recovered my voice and completed the poem. In spite of my lapse, my father was pleased with my performance and took me downtown and bought me an Elgin gold watch. However, he embarrassed me by making the salesman reduce the list price of the watch before he purchased it.

My younger brother Kenneth had the job of bringing in firewood and carrying out the ashes. I was put in charge of the chicken yard next to the barn and had the entire responsibility for it—buying the feed, cleaning out the roosts, and bringing the eggs to the kitchen, where I was paid twenty-five cents a dozen for them. I became more interested in chickens, subscribed to a poultry magazine, and bought a little book called *Standards of Perfection*, in which I learned that the best production strain of chickens for eggs were the Leghorns. Accordingly, I sold off my Plymouth Rock chickens and bought Leghorns of the rose-comb variety. I wanted to take a pen of my Leghorns, one cockerel and three pullets, to the Grand Western Livestock Show at Chicago in January 1899.

Mother let me use the laundry room in the basement to get my pen prepared to exhibit at the show. Following the directions in the book, I used one tub of soapy water to wash them, then a tub of clear water to rinse them, and finally a tub of water with blueing in it to give them a glossy white appearance. Then I rubbed vaseline on their beaks, wattles, and legs.

My mother loaned me a big straw picnic hamper to put them in for my trip to the Chicago fair. When I boarded the suburban train from Evanston to Chicago, the conductor made me leave the basket of chickens in the baggage car while I rode in the passenger coach. Halfway to Chicago, a brakeman came to the coach and called for the owner of the basket of chickens to come immediately to the baggage car. One of the mail clerks in the baggage car had gotten curious and opened the lid to the basket, and all the chickens had escaped and were flying all over the car. Some of them had settled on a casket and were busy scratching off the flowers and wreaths that rested upon it. After an exciting chase, the fowls were caught and put back in the basket, but in the scramble they had gotten so dusty that I knew they would never win any prizes. Nevertheless, I took them to the show and while there I met a breeder of rose-comb white Leghorns. He recognized the quality of my exhibit and offered me fifteen dollars for the pen. I sold it to him and brought the basket back home with me.

Though my Leghorns failed to win prizes, I always carried a great debt to them. Forty years later, my earlier efforts to apply standards of perfection to the chickens led me to pioneer the cause of performance testing to improve the Herefords on my ranch in Colorado and to become one of the founders of Performance Registry International.

In my sophomore year at Evanston High School I made the ice hockey team. In a scrimmage, my instep was cut and blood poisoning set in—a dangerous thing in the days before antibiotics. I was kept in bed for five weeks with my leg elevated. While Mother was worrying about my health, she talked with one of my teachers. His sister had married an Iowa farmer, G. A. Whitney, who had taken his wife and two young children to New Mexico to live on his recently acquired 20,000-acre ranch. My mother wrote Mrs. Whitney and she offered to board me on the ranch for twenty-five dollars a month.

I was thrilled with the idea of recuperating in the Wild West with no school to attend, though the Indians were long gone from eastern New Mexico and there were few cattle on the Whitney ranch, which was located in the foothills not far from Raton, New Mexico, on Caliente Creek, a tributary of the Vermejo River.

My adventure began in the summer of 1901, when my mother and I took the Santa Fe train from Chicago, bound for New Mexico. It was a three-day trip with stops at stations for meals. I never forgot my excitement as the train—taking on extra locomotives at La Junta, Colorado—moved slowly up Raton Pass with the Spanish Peaks rising to the west. We coasted down to Raton and left the train at Maxwell, where the Whitneys took us thirty miles in a spring wagon to the ranch through dazzling sunlight and the fragrance of sage, piñon, and juniper.

The Whitneys lived in a big adobe ranch house. Mother stayed one night and then returned to Illinois. Overnight I dropped into a new life that would hold charm for me for the rest of my days. In the fall, Mrs. Whitney took her children back to Iowa. That left me with Mr. Whitney and his two hired men, Marion and Lewis Brown, cousins who had gone west from Arkansas to learn the cowboy trade. I followed them wherever they went and copied everything they did. Soon I was writing letters home about living with cowboys wearing chaps and carrying a revolver, trapping coyotes with steel traps out near a prairie dog town, and chasing wild cattle. Every evening I spent in the Browns' room listening to their stories about boys who went west and became folk heroes in a Robin Hood way, taking money from the rich and giving it to the poor—heroes like Sam Bass, Jesse and Frank James, and Billy the Kid.

The Browns sang a lot, and I loved their songs about an eastern boy who hired out with a trail herd—and who, when he was about to die, did not want to be buried on the "Lone Prairie." Marion Brown said that when the trail herds went by that lonesome grave, the cowboys would scatter wildflowers on it. Often they mentioned the exploits of the great Texas drover, Charles Goodnight, who pioneered the Goodnight-Loving Trail in the late 1860s up the Pecos River and over Trinchera Pass into Colorado and on to Denver. The Browns claimed that Goodnight's trail ran right through Whitney's ranch on Caliente Creek.

Marion and Lewis Brown thought that they knew more about ranching than Mr. Whitney did. One day Marion said to me:

TOP: *The Carpenter family in Colorado Springs, about 1899. From left to right are Edward Farrington, Belle Reed, Ruth, Farrington, Kenneth, Willis Vincent, and nurse holding Marian.* BOTTOM: *From left to right are Bill Cross on Dan, Bruce Dawson with Paint, and Ferry Carpenter at 16 on Nugget.*

OPPOSITE PAGE

TOP: *John Barkley Dawson, 41, and third wife Lavinna, 31, at their wedding in 1871.* BOTTOM: *Jack White (left) and Ferry Carpenter with packhorse Sorry, ready to trade with Indians at Taos in 1904.*

"Kid, you are doing enough chores around here to pay for your board and room. Why don't you hit up the old man for a job?" I did so, and to my great delight Mr. Whitney agreed. I had the pleasure of writing my father that I was now on my *own* and he needn't send the twenty-five dollars a month board and room.

When Mrs. Whitney and the children returned from Iowa, she did not approve of the arrangement. She was penurious by nature and never could keep help in her kitchen. She had her husband take me away from outdoor cowboy work and made me put in my time as a kitchen maid washing dishes ("diving for pearls" the Browns called it), scrubbing floors, and doing a huge ranch laundry which had to be put through two large tubs of water drawn in a bucket from a well—one with hot, soapy suds and the other cold, clean rinse water. Both had to have all the clothes run through hand-powered wringers. The hardest part of this demotion for me to swallow was that I no longer had any cowboy tales to write home about.

One day, Marion Brown got an official letter from the General Land Office in Washington, saying that his homestead claim near Springer, New Mexico, was being contested and would be canceled unless he established residence on it immediately. That evening in the bunkhouse a scheme was hatched for all of us to quit work on the Whitney ranch and go in a body to Brown's homestead claim and develop it as an irrigated cattle ranch. Marion cautioned us all not to let a word of our plans get to the Whitneys until the day when we would all leave. "When you quit a job, always quit hard," he said, "for in that way they'll come to find out how indispensable you were."

Four days before the projected exodus, Mr. Whitney came to the kitchen, where I was working, and said he couldn't find either of the hired men. He wanted me to get on my pony, Nugget, and run in a Percheron mare by the name of Jewel. She was roughshod and running in the pasture with a stallion called Cub. When I ran my pony between them to start her for the barn, she wheeled and kicked me, breaking my left shinbone. I made it back to the house but had to be carried to bed. The Browns brought a doctor to the ranch from the nearby coal town of Dawson, and he set my broken leg in a cast. That happening postponed the day that had been set for all the help to leave the Whitneys.

Mrs. Whitney had a Singer sewing machine and she found out her youthful invalid could work the treadle on it with his good foot. She also had a closetful of sheets, pillow cases, and curtains that needed to be hemmed, and she had me sit where I could work the treadle on her machine while she fed articles into it.

By a former wife, Mr. Whitney had a grown son named Fred who had left the Caliente Ranch and married the daughter of a neighboring rancher named John B. Dawson. Dawson had sold part of his large ranch to the Phelps Dodge Company to operate a coal mine on Dawson property. J. B. Dawson was a legend in the region, a frontiersman who had seen service with the Texas Rangers fighting Indians. He had been a partner of Charles Goodnight, the trailblazer whom the Brown brothers had told me about.

Fred Whitney knew that I was discontented with my job on the Caliente and wrote me a letter saying that he had a contract to furnish a beef a day to the Phelps Dodge store at Dawson. He would give me my board and room if I would help him butcher his beef. He added that I would have no work to do that could not be done on horseback. That looked like an answer to a prayer, and as soon as I could ride, I left the Whitneys and reported to Fred, who was living with his father-in-law at the Dawson Ranch on the Vermejo River. The year was 1902.

That ranch was a unique establishment. Mr. Dawson had sold his coal rights to Phelps Dodge for $250,000 and had reserved a thousand-acre tract to live on. He had a son, Gus, by his first wife; two sons, Si and Bruce, by his second wife; and one son, Manly, by his third wife. The two daughters by his third wife were named after the first two wives.

There was a family story of how J. B. Dawson had met and married his third wife. Left a widower with three children from his first two wives, he was busily engaged in buying and selling cattle, and in a sparsely settled country he had little opportunity to meet eligible females. He heard about a widow in Trinidad, Colorado, who seemed to be the person he wanted. When the fall roundup was over, he set out by horse-drawn stage to go to Trinidad to meet her. On the two-day trip, he encountered a fellow passenger who was reading a religious periodical, *The Ram's Horn*, in the coach, and a poem in it appealed to Mr. Dawson. He forgot about the Trinidad widow and composed a letter to the lady author of the poem, telling her that it expressed beliefs that were his. He asked if he could come to Iowa where she lived and meet her with a view to matrimony.

When the letter came to Iowa from a strange man living in a remote country, it caused something of a sensation in the neighborhood. The mother of the poetess told her daughter not to answer the letter for a year, saying, "If that man is sincere, he will wait a year for an answer." When the year was over, she wrote Mr. Dawson and told him he could come to see her. He made the trip to Iowa and soon they were married. Bride and groom returned to the Dawson Ranch in New Mexico, where she became the beloved stepmother to Mr. Dawson's children by his two former wives.

The Dawson Ranch, where I worked in 1902, was typical of early-day ranching. It had a large adobe house where Mr. and Mrs. Dawson lived and where Fred Whitney and his wife had been assigned rooms. There was a long row of one-room apartments, each with an open fireplace, for warmth and cooking. Called "Poverty Row," this was open for relations and visitors who wanted to stay overnight, or maybe for a week or two. Everyone was welcome to go to the dining room in the big house and partake of the food, which was bountifully put on the table three times a day.

I always ate my noon meal there—and the first time, a small man with a black mustache sat at the table. He introduced himself as "Uncle Tom Curtis," a relative of Mr. Dawson. At his place was a glass of water containing his false teeth. These he called his "eating teeth," and he was wearing his "talking teeth." He exchanged teeth when it came time to eat. Finished eating, he put his eating teeth back in the glass and fished out his talking teeth for use until the next meal. The hired ranch hands, who were all Mexicans, ate in the "cook shack," where a man cook presided.

When I was not busy bringing in cattle for slaughter, or helping butcher them, I waited on Mr. Dawson. I caught and saddled his special mount, Old Coley, a black stallion. I rode with him and opened and shut the gates we went through. One day in the fall when the wild plums were ripe, he noticed fresh bear signs near the plum thicket. That was the signal for his annual bear hunt, to which he always invited his sons.

The hound dogs were shut up in a box stall in the barn and fed small rations of meat until they became ravenous, at which time they would fight among themselves over every bone. Mr. Dawson would say, "Fat dogs are poor hunters." On the first morning of the hunt, everyone was up and had their horses saddled before daylight. Each rider was given a pair of dogs necked together to lead on a rope. Only one dog was left untied. That dog was allowed to sound off and chase after every track encountered. As most of the tracks were of deer and rabbits, the dog exhausted himself before we came across bear tracks. When that happened, his bark changed from "Yip, yip" to a growl, and the hair on his back stood up. We were all cautioned not to unfasten our pair of dogs until Mr. Dawson, as master of the hunt, gave the signal. We must also not let the dogs get away while necked, because they might hang up in some brush.

When the lead dog started to follow a bear track, Mr. Dawson motioned to all to turn the dogs loose. I was so excited that I let mine go still coupled. I was afraid to admit it, so I hoped they would not hang up and die somewhere. It was thrilling to hear the whole pack go off baying on the trail, and to watch the riders following them. Mr. Dawson did not join in the stampede, and to my chagrin, he told me not to go with the others. He said that the bear trail led up a box canyon where the bears went to sleep after gorging on the plums. When the dogs aroused the bears, he said, they would be unable to leave the canyon because of the rimrock around its head. They would run back towards the thickets on the river.

We sat and listened until the baying of the dogs could not be heard. After about fifteen minutes, we began to hear faint barking, which increased as it got nearer to us. All of a sudden, a black bear followed by a pack of dogs burst out of a thicket near us. When the animal saw us, it scrambled up a piñon tree. The dogs circled the tree and barked and jumped at it, but the bear was safe from them. Mr. Dawson dismounted and took his three-barreled gun out of the holder. With one shot he killed the bear, and it came tumbling to the ground, where all the dogs pounced on it. He told me to help him keep the dogs away, opened up the bear, and began skinning it as casually as we skinned an animal in the butcher pen at the ranch. When the other hunters arrived, they all had to admit that Mr. Dawson was the best hunter.

Another of the big yearly events on the Dawson Ranch was the fall roundup, when the fat cattle were gathered and shipped for market. As a tenderfoot, I was not asked to go on this mission. After the roundup I heard stories of a wild red cow with a broken horn called Sally Jenkins, which the Dawson cowboys simply could not gather. She escaped them by jumping fifteen-foot gulches and hiding in thickets too dense for a horse to enter.

When spring came, Bruce Dawson invited me to go on the spring roundup. Bruce assigned me two extra mounts besides my own horse, Nugget. I rode with a fine roper, John Littrell. To my delight, John got his rope on Sally Jenkins. I roped her hind feet and we stretched her out on the ground. The customary procedure was to dehorn her, which John did by breaking off the horns with a large rock. That done, she could not gore horse or rider. Next John propped her eyelids open with twigs. A cow that cannot close her eyes will not run into the brush and can be driven with the herd. Finally, taking a hunting knife, John severed the tendon in her front knees. She could walk normally, but when she tried to run, the knees collapsed and she would tumble to the ground. After several attempts at escape, when we let her up, she became resigned to her fate and joined the herd, no longer a wild cow. Such was ranch life in New Mexico in the summer of 1903.

At the end of my second summer at the Dawson Ranch, I went back for my third year at Evanston Township High School. My old friend, Jack White, and I could not wait to get back West but felt we should tackle something more profitable than working for board and room on a ranch where we got the blame for everything that went wrong and seldom got credit for our accomplishments. We decided to find a more exciting way to spend our vacation during the summer of 1904.

At the Caliente, Marion Brown had told me about an isolated Indian pueblo called Taos where the inhabitants had a lot of buffalo hides and beaver pelts, which they would sell cheap because they had no nearby market to take them to. He said they would not accept paper currency in payment but would sell anything for silver money.

That sounded like the kind of "do-it" idea my father would approve of. I joined Jack in Kansas and we worked all June near Dodge City, harvesting wheat for good wages. We saved our money and I borrowed two hundred dollars from my father. The venture took us to Taos to invest in hides and pelts that we knew would sell for a big profit if we could get them to a railway station.

We bought three worn-out harvest horses cheap and rode them to Marion Brown's place near Springer, New Mexico. We had our own saddles and purchased one extra horse to pack our bedding and camp equipment. When we got to Taos after a three-day trip up the Cimarron past Eagle Nest, we camped on a creek outside Taos Pueblo.

The pueblo consisted of a number of buildings, one on top of the other. The town was enclosed by a four-foot adobe wall, and we were told that any trouble we might get into if inside that wall would be tried by Indian authorities and not by American courts. The usual punishment for misdemeanors was to tie the culprit to a post and let the Indian children use him as a target for their bow and arrow practice.

When we entered the pueblo on foot, our pockets sagging with silver coins, we found that neither did the Indians understand English nor we their dialect. We finally found a young Indian who had graduated from the Carlisle Indian School in Pennsylvania, and he acted as our interpreter and counselor. He said there were very few buffalo hides in the pueblo and the beaver had been trapped out of the river fifteen years ago.

There were, he said, some products made in Taos Pueblo that were of mercantile value. These were vases, plates, pitchers, and cups—all manufactured by the Indian women from a seam of red clay, baked in a community furnace, and then decorated with black letters and signs. There was no local market for them, and we easily purchased all we could get into our pack outfit to take to Raton, where the Santa Fe tourist trains stopped for dinner at the Harvey House. The Indians displayed their rugs and blankets at that station, and we were assured that if we dressed up as Indians and painted our faces, we could readily sell our pottery to the passengers.

The only problem was how to transport our purchases to Raton's passenger platform. We decided to wrap each utensil with dry grass held on by strings and put all our vases in our bedrolls in such a way that they would be underneath our packhorse's belly. This horse we called Sorry because of his disconsolate expression. He had a habit of stumbling, which we planned to guard against by taking turns leading him by hand and keeping one hand under his chin so he would not fall down.

Wandering around the pueblo one day, we came across a big hole in the ground with a kind of canopy over it. Though we did not know what it was at the time, it was a kiva, a sacred place for religious and tribal council meetings. Out of curiosity Jack started down the ladder of the kiva, when an old Indian in a breechclout jumped out of the blackness and went after Jack with a knife in his hand. Jack came up the ladder in a hurry and we both ran for the wall around the pueblo. Not stopping to unlatch the gate, we just bolted over the top of the wall.

We thought it best not to return to Taos Pueblo. Having no further business there, we set out for Raton with Sorry and another horse. It was slow going, leading the packhorse by hand, and we got to quarreling as to whose turn it was to walk and hold up Sorry's head. Near Eagle Nest was a little mountain lake, and on it were some ducks. We decided to have duck for dinner but could not agree on whose turn it was to shoot our .22 caliber rifle. Dropping the bridle reins and hackamore lead rope on the ground, we let the horses graze while we walked together to the lake. Unbeknownst to us was a tall rimrock noted for the wonderful echo it gave to any noise. When we shot the duck, the echo sounded like a clap of thunder and so scared our horses that they stampeded off together, dragging their reins and the lead rope. There happened to be a pole bridge over the gulch, and although both saddle horses got over it all right, Sorry put one foot through the poles and fell flat down through them with the crashing noise of broken pottery. No piece bigger than a silver dollar was left of our two-hundred-dollar investment.

All that was left for us to do was to get back to Marion Brown's place at Springer and take the train back to Chicago to be ready for school. Since we had no money, on Marion's advice we raffled our horses, saddles, and camp outfit all over Springer. The effort brought us nearly a hundred dollars, which was not enough to buy two full-fare tickets to Chicago, so we decided to get one full-fare and one half-fare ticket for children under twelve. The ticket agent asked who the half fare was for, and I pointed to Jack, who was four inches shorter than I.

"How old are you?" the agent asked Jack.

"Eleven," Jack replied.

"The hell you are," the agent snorted. "You can't put that over on me."

Nonplussed, we walked back to Marion's camp for the night. He said he would help us with the agent, who was a disagreeable kind of fellow. We followed Marion into the depot the next day, and he told the agent he had known Jack since he was a baby; that he was a bit overgrown, but was only eleven years old.

Marion was not the kind of man who anyone wanted to get into a fight with, so the agent sold us the full-fare and half-fare tickets but remarked that he hoped the conductor would throw Jack off the train when it was going sixty miles an hour. That threat caused us some more worry, and we decided not to go on the day train but to wait for the Midnight Flyer.

This train did not regularly stop at Springer but would do so if a red signal light was hung out for it to stop. The agent hung the light out and then locked up the station and left us to shiver in the cold night air until the Midnight Flyer got in. When it came, only one vestibule was open for passengers, and we rushed back to get in. The conductor had a lantern on his arm. When I handed him the two tickets, one blue, one yellow, he said, "Who is the half fare for?" I pointed behind me to Jack, but when I looked back, he had squatted down until he was only three feet high.

"Get on, get on," the conductor yelled. We ran back to the tourist sleepers and had enough money to pay for an upper berth, which was all made up. Jack climbed in, boots and all, and got under the covers before the conductor came through. There he had to remain until we got to Chicago, while I explained that he was not feeling well.

When we got back to Evanston, we had nothing to show except a bow and arrows and buckskin leggings we had purchased from our Indian interpreter. It was several years before we were able to pay my father the two hundred dollars we had borrowed from him.

TWO

Charles Goodnight and Mr. Dawson's Baptism

The next summer, 1905, I again went to the Dawson Ranch. I met a young easterner on a roundup on Cimarron Creek. He had been threatened with tuberculosis and had been sent by his family to Maxwell to recover his health. I told him that I was getting bored with high school and was not planning to go to college. He replied that I was making a big mistake. He said that he had graduated from Lawrenceville School, a prep school in New Jersey, and had spent a semester at Princeton University before his health broke down.

"You must go to college," he said, "but don't pick a college by its football team or its campus buildings. Select one headed by an educator of status. Such a man," he went on, "has been elected president of Princeton University. His name is Woodrow Wilson, and he has made big improvements already in the Princeton curriculum."

Back in Evanston that fall of 1905, I was able with some tutoring to pass the College Entrance Board examinations and was admitted to Princeton, class of 1909, without having graduated from high school. My father was pleased with my choice and agreed to pay all my expenses for the four college years.

While adjusting to life in New Jersey as a Princeton freshman, I thought often of something Mr. Dawson had told me when the Phelps Dodge Company built a spur line through his ranch from the Santa Fe Railroad to the coal town of Dawson.

"I've lived all my life on the frontier," Mr. Dawson had said, "and now I don't want to spend the rest of it next door to a coal camp where a coal tipple keeps locomotive whistles going twenty-four hours a day."

When I heard from Mr. Dawson next, he wrote that he was preparing to escape from railroads by moving from New Mexico to a 2,000-acre ranch that he had purchased in Routt County, Colorado.

"Colorado is a new country," he wrote, "and the place for a young man to go. The public domain is all open and unfenced. Any citizen over twenty-one years of age can file on a homestead and, by living on it seven months a year for five years, can get title to 160 acres of free land. The hills out there are full of deer and elk and antelope, and the streams are full of trout."

I couldn't get that alluring picture of Colorado out of my mind. I wrote and asked Mr. Dawson for a summer job. He replied that he would give me one with board and room if I could find my way to his new Colorado ranch. I looked up Routt County in the Princeton library and found that it extended from the Continental Divide near a place called Steamboat Springs 150 miles west to the Utah border. From the Wyoming line the county ran 75 miles south nearly to the Grand River (now the Colorado). Its area in 1906 was 4,458,880 acres, which made it larger than the states of Connecticut and Rhode Island together. Routt County was named in 1877 for John L. Routt, the first governor of the new state of Colorado. Its total population in 1900 was 3,600. The post office address of Mr. Dawson's new ranch was Hayden, a village on the Yampa River, 22 miles from Steamboat Springs. Hayden was named for F. V. Hayden, who had surveyed the region for the government in 1874.

There was no railroad in Routt County yet, though I learned that David Moffat was building one from Denver across Middle Park headed for Salt Lake City. The Princeton librarian found for me a copy of Professor Hayden's *Atlas for Colorado*, dated 1877. The multicolored map showed me that Mr. Dawson's Hayden was in a truly frontier country. A single road from Denver ran some 250 miles across Berthoud Pass and Middle Park to the Grand River and then over the Gore Range to the Yampa River and so on to Hayden. All the Hayden area was designated "coal lands" by Hayden's map. Westward from there along the Yampa for a hundred miles, not a single town was shown on the map and the land was marked "sage and bad lands."

In June 1906, at the end of my freshman year at Princeton, my father bought my rail ticket from Evanston to Denver, where I found that the only way that Hayden could be reached was to take the Denver and Rio Grande Railroad to a place called Wolcott, Colorado, and from there by horse-drawn stage to Hayden. Because of the high Continental Divide west of Denver, the train looped far out of its way south to Pueblo and north again through the Royal Gorge and over Tennessee Pass to Wolcott on Eagle River.

I was the only passenger on the all-night train to Wolcott. At the small Wolcott depot I saw a Concord stagecoach and two men loading a big pile of mail sacks just thrown out of the baggage car into the back rack of the stagecoach. I asked the white-haired old driver if he would sell me a ticket to Hayden.

"Hell, no," he responded. "I only go as far as Yampa, and there are two other stages that have the mail contracts from there to Steamboat Springs, and on down the Yampa River to Hayden and Craig. I'll sell you a ticket to Yampa."

There were no other passengers when I looked inside the windows of the coach, so I asked the driver, who told me his name was Dave, if I could sit on top with him.

"Yes, you can," Dave replied, "if there ain't no schoolmarms, but if there is, she will ride up there with me, and you'll ride right in there." He pointed towards the inside of the coach. I climbed up on the top seat beside Dave. He had an iron brake to brace himself with his foot and a fistful of reins to steady his body when the coach rolled backwards and forwards on the rawhide strips on which it was mounted. We had not gone far when he let the horses break into a gallop going down a hill, and the coach rocked forward and backward and sideways as we went from one rut to another in the road. I had nothing to hold on to when this happened, so I threw my arm around Dave and hugged him. He smiled and said, "That's why I give schoolmarms a preference in riding up here with me. They have to hug me or fall off."

We stopped at the McCoy post office, fifteen miles from Wolcott, to change horses and to get a noon meal. Mrs. McCoy's inn was famous for its comfort and hospitality. The owner had the table loaded with wild meat and vegetables from her garden. Three young surveyors joined us when we left McCoys and they all sat inside the coach.

When we got to the wide main street of Yampa, Dave cracked his whip and we went in on a gallop, wheeling around to the front of the drugstore where the post office was. It looked like the whole town had gathered there to greet us, and I felt that this was as thrilling as Buffalo Bill's show.

As Yampa was the end of the line for that coach, and a new one to Steamboat Springs did not leave until the next day, the passengers all lined up at the Antlers Hotel in Yampa for a room to stay in overnight. I got the last available room, and the young surveyor who was behind me in the line was told there were no more rooms to let.

"I'm a stranger and you'll have to take care of me," he said.

"No chance," replied the clerk, "unless you are willing to sleep with the redheaded school teacher."

The surveyor said firmly, "*I* am a gentleman."

"So's he," replied the clerk.

The next day, with a new stage driver, I rode on to Steamboat Springs, the largest town in Routt County. It was an all-day, thirty-five-mile trip, stopping to change horses and get a noon meal in a beautiful grassy interval called Oak Creek.

The driver told me that Steamboat Springs was noted for its many medicinal and natural hot springs. It had a large wooden bathhouse where hot sulphur water provided for eight private bathrooms and a large wooden swimming pool. On my third day out of Wolcott with another driver and a new coach, we left Steamboat at eight in the morning and arrived at the Scottie Locknane Cabin at Tow Creek, called the Halfway House, by noon to change horses and get dinner. There were no screens on either the doors or windows, and the only way guests could eat their food was when a kitchen attendant pulled a long lath, hung from the ceiling with a paper fringe on it, back and forth to keep the flies off the food. When the girl operator was called to the kitchen to get more food, and the lath and hanger lay still, the flies immediately covered all the food on the table and plates. Eating a meal there was a kind of contest between the flies and the boarders.

In the afternoon the stage rounded a big sandstone bluff called Gibraltar Rock, and when we crossed the wide, rippling Yampa River the meadows of the Dawson Ranch came into view. The driver let me off five miles short of Hayden, at the end of a half-mile lane to Mr. Dawson's headquarters.

During my ninety-mile stage journey from Wolcott to Hayden, my drivers had posted me on where I was—how entry into Routt County from the east was blocked by the high Continental Divide with passes like Rabbit Ears at 9,680 feet and the difficult Gore Pass road from Middle Park to Yampa and Hayden. Because of the barrier posed by the Rockies and the hostility of the Ute Indians prior to their removal in 1881, the earliest of what would become Routt County pioneers came down the Green River in the 1830s first to Brown's Park near Utah and later, in 1870, from the Union Pacific lines at Rawlins, Wyoming.

As I walked up the lane toward the Dawson ranch house and buildings, I thought how much better this magnificent Western Slope country of Colorado suited my temperament than New Mexico with its monotonous plains stretching away to the blue horizon in west Texas. As Mr. Dawson had written, Colorado was a young man's country, a challenging place for someone like me who was eager to get up and do something.

When I arrived at the Dawson Ranch I found to my surprise that Mr. Dawson had gone into the business of raising mules. Mules are hybrid animals, a cross between a mare and a donkey, with neither pride of ancestry nor hope of posterity. They have more stamina and common sense than horses. When a runaway team of mules comes to a barbed wire gate, they stop instead of plunging into it as a team of horses would do, cutting themselves up on the wire.

Mr. Dawson had two jacks, one black and the other grey, and about seventy-five brood mares that he was breeding to the jacks. My first job that summer of 1906 was to take care of the jacks, which were kept in separate stables. I was told never to let them get together because they would fight until one got the better of the other, throwing it on the ground by sinking his teeth like a bulldog into its neck and never letting go until it fell and could be trampled on. Coming and going around the jacks, I carried a broom with me, for jacks have long and sensitive ears and are afraid of having them brushed by a broom.

It was all new to me but very interesting. Every morning I brought the mares to the corral and turned in with them an "original" gelding (one not completely castrated, called a "teaser") to find out if a mare was ready to be bred. Our teaser was a one-testicled stallion called George. When George located a mare ready to be bred, I grabbed his long halter rope and led him away before he could act. Then I put the mare in a wooden stock to hold her and brought in the jack for service. Mares are afraid of jacks with their loud braying and prancing around. The mare has to wear a blind bridle to keep her from seeing the jack. I became expert at this work and prided myself on my ability.

Mr. Dawson had no cattle at Hayden, but sold surplus hay to his three sons, who ran cattle summertime on the public land or on leased state lands. Frank Curtis, a nephew of Mr. Dawson, was in charge of all cattle owned by any member of the family. He had a cow camp in a lovely spot south of Hayden called Twenty Mile Park. It was a great treat for me to be sent out to stay with him for a week or so and attend the roundups when the new calves were branded.

Frank was a kindly man who loved any sort of animal. He had a host of pet chipmunks around his cabin that came at mealtime to be fed. One little chipmunk ran across the lid of a hot Dutch oven and cauterized all four paws. Frank called it Stumpy because it ran around on its four stump legs.

Frank Curtis was a top hand with cattle. He taught me the basic rules of range herding—how to ride fence, keep gates shut, cook outdoors, and prevent the bulls from congregating in bachelor groups at water holes. He took me with him to my first roundup in Routt County. We each rode a horse and led a packhorse with our beds on them. When we reported to the roundup boss, the man told us where to put our beds and what part of the country we were to ride.

Frank warned me not to be critical of what I saw. In New Mexico, all regular cowboys used a double-cinch saddle, and many of these sported silver conchos. Rawhide and braided hair bridles were customary—and often long-braided reins with a quirt on the end of them. Spade bits were common, and no one ever came without silver-decorated spurs and leather chaperaroes. In the Routt County roundups, on the other hand, some of the cattle owners came bareback on old work horses with blind bridles, and none of them had the professional dress and style noticeable at roundups in New Mexico. Frank explained to me that the Coloradans were homesteaders or small ranchmen and spent little time on a horse. "Don't fool yourself about their being cowmen," he added, "for that part is just a side issue to their farm work."

Among other accomplishments, I learned from Frank how to bury a calf's head, with the hide on, into a pit of hot coals, and then to cover it with dirt and let it cook for six hours. When it was then dug up and the hide peeled off, we could find tender, tasty meat on the cheekbones. The old-timers always considered the eyes the choicest bits of meat and used their long-bladed jackknives, which were about three or four inches long, to gouge them out.

Mrs. Dawson was a devoted member of the hard-shell Baptist church. When she was in New Mexico she used to have a minister of that faith come to the ranch and hold a week of services. Mr. Dawson had never been to school. He had difficulty reading, and his wife taught him how to sign his name instead of using a symbolic figure. He had never joined the church or been baptized.

One summer Mr. Dawson decided to join the church, which required complete immersion for baptism. A day was set for this ceremony and all the relations far and near were invited to come for a week's visit and witness the conversion and baptism.

I was writing most of Mr. Dawson's correspondence for him. One day he said to me, "Ferry, take a letter." He dictated it as follows:

> Charles Goodnight, Goodnight, Texas.
> Friend Charles,
>   On August 5, I will go down to the watery grave and would like you to be there.

Mr. Goodnight had been Mr. Dawson's partner in their cattle trailing days before Goodnight set up his famous million-acre JA Ranch at Palo Duro Canyon, the first ranch in the Texas Panhandle. Goodnight was a man of seventy years in 1906 and a legendary figure in all of Texas.

When I finished the letter to Goodnight, Mr. Dawson said, "Now give me a pen and I'll sign the letter." He made the first letter of his name, and then got confused and threw the pen on the floor.

TOP: *Buffalo, cattalo, elk, and antelope in pasture at Dawson Ranch on north side of Yampa River, about 1908.* BOTTOM: *Stage at Gibraltar Rock, six miles east of Hayden, about 1903.*

OPPOSITE PAGE

TOP LEFT: *Charles Goodnight, 92, with second wife Corinne, whom he married in 1927. He died on December 12, 1929.* TOP RIGHT: *Frank Curtis (left) and Marion Curtis, nephews of John Dawson, about 1904.* CENTER LEFT: *Baptism of John Dawson, 1906.* BOTTOM: *Dawson Ranch, about 1916. Square building at left is the ice house, at right the well and pump house. The mule barn is to the rear.*

"Ferry, go to the barn and get a branding iron," he said. "I can write better with it than with this pen."

In due time a reply came from Mr. Goodnight saying he would come up for the baptism, and that in honor of the occasion he was sending as a present to Mr. Dawson a railroad car with two full-blooded buffalo bulls, five full-blooded buffalo cows, three with calves at side, and the rest of the car filled with Galloway and Angus cows. When this shipment reached Wolcott, Frank Curtis, Pete Wilkinson, and I were sent to drive the buffalo and cattle to the ranch at Hayden. It was a difficult task, as they would not stay together. The only way a buffalo could be turned was to surround it with domestic cattle, and then turn the collection together.

After some days of trailing the buffalo, we managed to get them to the ranch where we found extensive preparations going on for the baptism. The Burlins, relatives from Texas, drove up in a covered wagon and camped in the front yard. Mrs. Dawson sent to Denver and got a woman cook for the period—a big red-headed woman who was given a bedroom adjoining the kitchen. When she found that I went to Hayden horseback each day to get the mail, she told me to ask for letters for Mrs. Worthington, Mrs. Olin, and Mrs. Barnes. She said she had been married three times, but all her husbands had died. Two of them were Civil War veterans, and she got a pension check for each of them every three months. The third husband had been a Rebel, she said, and although she liked him the best of the three, she did not get a pension check for him. "Don't tell nobody this," she cautioned me.

I asked Frank Curtis why Mr. Dawson had decided to get baptized in the cold water of the Yampa River. He said, "Uncle John has always been a farsighted man in his dealings. He thinks this is the cheapest insurance he can get. But if he sneezes when he comes up, it won't take."

A week before the service, Mr. Goodnight himself came on the Denver and Rio Grande Railroad to Wolcott, and I was sent over with a top buggy and two mules to bring him to the ranch. It took me two days of hard driving each way to make the trip. Mr. Goodnight was a huge, forbidding-looking old gentleman, but he was a keen observer of the country. He was an ardent believer in crossing the buffalo with his native Texas cows and he called the offspring "cattaloes." He told me that they would withstand the flies in West Texas better than cattle and would never drift like cattle do in a storm. "They just face a storm, drop their big curly heads to the ground, shut their eyes and face it," he said.

When I delivered Mr. Goodnight to the ranch, Mr. Dawson told me to obey any order he might give me. If he wanted a horse to ride or a buggy or a team, I was to get it for him pronto. For many hours, I posted myself in a room where Mr. Goodnight was telling tales of the old days when he fought the Comanche Indians in Texas. He explained that the Comanches had two techniques in warfare. One was the ambush, in which they concealed themselves for a surprise attack; the other was the frontal charge, whereby they ran their horses straight into the enemy's position. In one fight, Mr. Goodnight said, two of his men turned tail during a charge. Mr. Dawson asked what happened to them, and Mr. Goodnight replied, "I shot them." After that disclosure, I lost no time in carrying out any orders Mr. Goodnight saw fit to give me.

When the baptismal meetings were ready to begin, three preachers arrived to conduct them—Elder Howard from Kansas, Brother Thompson from Trinidad, and Brother Fetter from Raton. Halfway through the week of services, a small, white-haired gentleman joined us and said he was a licensed Baptist minister. He was welcomed in, and soon took a leading part in the services. The main theme of his talks was about how mankind could not remain Christianized, and always went back to former habits. To emphasize this he would quote from the Bible the verse about the dog returning to its vomit.

One morning I got up early, and when I looked out at the end of the lane where the mail coach went by every morning, I saw Brother Howard standing there to meet the stage. I asked Bruce Dawson where he was going. "Didn't you hear about it?" Bruce said. "Ma got up this morning to get breakfast started, and when she looked in the red-headed cook's bedroom to get her up, she found Brother Howard in bed with her. She ordered him off the ranch, and that's why he's down there to catch the stage."

When Sunday came, Mr. Dawson woke me early and told me to ride across the river and invite all the neighbors to come to the baptismal ceremony. A feast was prepared and all were invited to partake of it.

After two hours of services indoors, we all marched down to the riverbank. Fred Whitney, my old boss at the Caliente ranch in New Mexico and Mr. Dawson's son-in-law, was there. He called me aside and said, "Ferry, Mr. Dawson is a pretty heavy old man, and those Baptist preachers are pretty light. He might get away from them in the river current when he goes under." He then opened his coat and handed me a lariat he had concealed there, and said, "Take this and stand downstream. If he gets away from them, you lasso him."

When Mr. Dawson was waist-deep in the river, two preachers stood on opposite sides of him with their hands on his head. They prayed awhile and then signaled to the women who were on the bank, and they sang. I wondered why the preachers in the river did not finish the ceremony. One of them kept looking at the sky and all at once a shaft of sunlight broke through a cloud and struck right on Mr. Dawson's head. Elder Fetter raised his hand and said, "God in heaven welcomes this old pioneer into his Kingdom." Then he signaled the rancher to fall over backward. As Mr. Dawson disappeared under the water, the silence was intense. Then we heard three-year-old John Dawson, who was in his father's arms, yell, "Oh, see Granpa bubble!"

The old man waded to the shore, dripping wet, and each one of his sons in order of age went up and embraced and kissed him.

"Ferry," said Gus, the oldest son, "you go up and kiss him after Bruce." It got me wet to do so, but I felt honored to be allowed to salute him as his sons had, so I followed suit.

Mr. Dawson then walked slowly back to the ranch house, changed his clothes, and sat on the porch to receive greetings from all of those assembled. The wrinkles on his face seemed to be less deep, and his countenance had a lift to it that was rarely seen. I'm sure most of the onlookers like myself felt that he had indeed entered into a new life.

One of the congregation, Annie Elmer, had come over on horseback to be present. She had a Brownie Kodak and took pictures of the ceremony which she afterward let me make copies of.

Mr. Goodnight stayed over a couple of nights after the baptism, while I attended a roundup on the Little Snake River the next day. When I mentioned that Charles Goodnight was visiting at the Dawson Ranch, Ike Kelo, the roundup captain who was a Texas boy, rode horseback twenty-five miles to the ranch at night, as he said, "just to shake hands with Uncle Charlie."

I drove a team and buggy with Mr. Goodnight back to Wolcott. I wanted him to talk about more Indian fights, but he kept the conversation on matters concerned with the adaptability of the country for cattle raising and the benefits of crossbreeding the buffalo and native cattle. When he got back to Texas, he sent me a photograph of himself and his second wife, who was his nurse after Mrs. Goodnight's death. She was a widow thirty-five years old. And believe it or not the young widow had a baby when Goodnight was well past seventy. The child lived only a year, but its advent was a matter of pride to Mr. Goodnight's admirers all over Texas.

THREE

Woodrow Wilson

When I had returned home to Evanston in early September 1905, full of stories about Marion Brown and Sally Jenkins, the wild cow, Mother worried about outfitting me properly for starting my freshman year at Princeton. She consulted with the mothers of Princeton boys in the neighborhood, packed away my big hat, high-heeled boots, spurs, and tattered Levis, and put me into high stiff collars, vested suits, and neckties.

Since my father had business in Boston, we went east together on the Pennsy from Chicago and I disembarked at Princeton Junction, where a shuttle car would take me three miles to the campus. My father had never advised me much on how to live but had assigned that task to Mother. However, before I left the train, he said to me, "There will be a lot of rich young men in Princeton that will attract a number of no-good girls. I don't want you to have anything to do with them, but if you do and get one of them into trouble, come to me and don't get mixed up with some quack."

When I got to Princeton, I rented a room at 2 Nassau Street, signed in at Nassau Hall, and got a handbook entitled *The Freshman Bible*, which told me that the fancy clothes Mother had bought for me were all wrong. A freshman had to wear a black turtleneck sweater, corduroy trousers, and a little black cap called a "dink" on the back of his head. When I toured the campus, I learned that the first two weeks of the fall term were given over to "horsing" of freshmen by sophomores to teach them the traditions of the institution.

One evening some sophomores took me to one of their eating places and had me stand on a dining room chair and give my school yell. They assumed that I had prepped at Andover or Lawrenceville or some such eastern school. I did not know if Evanston High School had a yell. Winning games in Evanston had seemed tame to me compared to capturing outlaw cows like Sally Jenkins. So I just said, "Rah, rah, Evanston Township High School." That got no applause and when another freshman, Ferdinand Sanford made up a yell, he got so much more merriment than I had that I was allowed to go home. Sanford's yell was:

> Lily, laly, lily, lay,
> Lilies bloom in the month of May,
> Hippity hop, flippity flop,
> Who's on top? Warwick Seminary!

Ferdinand Sanford afterwards became an eminent jurist in Syracuse, New York, but from then on his classmates always called him Lily.

For another "horsing," I was marched down the middle of Nassau Street with a cap pistol in my hand which I kept firing at another freshman named Harry Trimble, who walked backward in front of me. Every time I fired the pistol, Harry would say, "Don't shoot! I'll marry the girl." I also was entered in what was called "Circus Maximus," which took place in a grass plot near the railroad station. Two naked freshmen linked together ran a sort of chariot race on their hands and knees. The winners could go home but the losers had to race again. I became good at running on all fours.

One day the front door of 2 Nassau Street was flung open by a junior who shouted, "All out, freshmen, for the Cannon Rush." Down the street in columns of eight came freshmen marching under the leadership of juniors who carried torches. They were all singing:

> Oh, we'll whoop it up for oughty-nine,
> We'll whoop it up again

We'll whoop it up for oughty-nine,
A jolly set of men.

I joined their ranks, and for the first time in my life felt the
thrill of being in a body of boys my age all banded together in a
common cause.

The march brought us to an old Revolutionary War cannon on
campus that was stuck open and down in the ground. A sophomore was standing on top of it while his classmates circled
around to prevent the freshmen from setting their champion on
the cannon and knocking the sophomore off. The crush and
cheers were so distracting that I couldn't tell what was going on,
until suddenly a junior yelled, "All over freshmen. Run home."
There was a similar battle on another night called the "Cane
Spree," in which freshmen and sophomore champions struggled
to get sole possession of a cane.

The most impressive event in my freshman year was Woodrow
Wilson's reception for the new class, which was held at Prospect,
the imposing residence of the college's president. Horsing was
called off for that evening so freshmen could get across the campus to Prospect without being bothered.

I attended with the other boys from 2 Nassau Street. We were
all introduced to President Wilson, his beautiful wife, and his
three daughters. It was the first time I had ever seen him, though
I had heard much about him. He was a tall, slender man with a
long, pale, ascetic face and a keen, alert expression. Born a Vir-
ginian, he was approaching fifty years of age in 1905, had attended Princeton himself (class of '79), and had taught at Bryn
Mawr, Wesleyan, and Johns Hopkins before joining the Princeton faculty in 1890. In 1902 he was elected president of
Princeton, replacing Francis L. Patton on grounds of Patton's
inefficiency and indifference to high academic standards.
Politically Wilson was called a "progressive," though only close
friends knew that he held political ambitions. While upgrading
the Princeton curriculum, Wilson tightened campus discipline
and expressed the wish to rid the college of its reputation as the
"finest country club in America."

At Prospect, refreshments were served—ice cream and cake.
When I took my plate and went by an open window to eat, a
sophomore with a big orange ribbon on his hat jumped from the
bushes near the window and, pointing a finger at me, said: "I've

got you spotted, freshman. Hand me that dish of ice cream and cake." I did so and stayed away from the open windows after getting a second helping.

President Wilson made a short address of welcome to the freshmen that evening that I never forgot. He made us feel as though we were in quest of the Holy Grail and were to have a chance to join the long line of prominent men who had helped to fashion the Republic. When we got back to our rooms, we talked about it, and all of us agreed to go and listen to him whenever we could, whether it was a student gathering or any other occasion. If he went down to Trenton to talk, we cut classes and took the rickety trolley car there to hear him.

My class of 1909 was the first to get the benefit in our freshman year of Wilson's new preceptorial method of instruction, copied after the tutorial method used at Oxford in England. It consisted of an informal gathering of not more than five or six students with a professor to discuss the subject that the students were taking. It was characterized in a faculty song which the seniors sang on the steps of Nassau Hall on evenings in the spring:

> Here's to them Preceptor guys,
> Fifty stiffs to make us wise.
> Easy work and lots of pay,
> Work the students night and day.

The next time I heard Woodrow Wilson speak was when he came to the Whig Literary Society to give an informal talk to students who were planning to go to law school. Princeton had two literary societies, Whig and Clio halls, each with a classical Greek-style building, side by side on the campus. Whig had been founded by James Madison and Clio by Aaron Burr when they were undergraduates.

That evening President Wilson gave two pieces of advice. He recommended that as undergraduates we begin to assemble a library of our own. Instead of going to the college library to read a book that was cited for reference in a course, he said, we should buy the book. Then, as we read it, we were to make pencil marks in the passages that impressed us. He said a book with marginal notations was like a tool that had been sharpened. I wrote my father about that advice, because I knew that buying books would be costly. In his reply, he advised me to do just that, and he would gladly pay the additional cost.

The other of Woodrow Wilson's recommendations was aimed at prospective law students. He advised us to take as many subjects as possible that would broaden our knowledge of life, such as the English classics. He went on to say that the study of law caused minds to be precise in the use of words, and the best chance to understand the pa, he quoted a well-known judge, who, when he was in college, took a course in Greek art to enlighten himself on ancient civilization. I liked that advice because I was poor at mathematics and enjoyed reading history, so I elected to take courses in history, politics, and economics.

The doors to Whig and Clio were always locked, and the only way to open them was to know the combination. All freshmen were given a chance to join one or the other of these societies. I chose Whig—the one begun by James Madison. I knew President Wilson had been a member of Whig when he was a student at Princeton.

The initiation into the society was noted for its secrecy. I dressed for the occasion in a sweater and corduroy trousers. After being blindfolded and led into innumerable rooms to be instructed about the goals and aims of the society, I had to crawl through a small tunnel that would eventually lead me to escape. Before getting to the end, I had to sign my name on a register in red ink, supposedly the blood of the founder. As I left, I was handed a small object to put in my pocket and was told not to examine it until I was back in my room, but I looked at it as soon as I got outside. It was a small, white cylindrical china insulator such as are used to attach electric wires to poles. On it was the inscription: "Preserve this section of the petrified penis of our great founder, James Madison!"

All Princeton students had to attend morning chapel exercises twice a week. To monitor attendance, the student had to sign a card and leave it at the door with a white-haired old gentleman whom the students always referred to as Saint Peter. At one chapel exercise, President Wilson unexpectedly presided. When he repeated the Lord's Prayer, he got part of it mixed up, and the students all began to shuffle their feet, raising a lot of dust and noise. President Wilson looked startled, and when he realized what the cause of this was, he closed the big Bible and stalked off the platform without closing the service.

Woodrow Wilson believed that one of the best ways to keep the undergraduates interested in their studies was for the president of the college to teach a class. He taught two subjects in my sophomore year, one in constitutional government and one in jurisprudence. His courses were popular because he was recognized as a master of these subjects and a compelling speaker. He did not allow us to take notes ("I don't like to lecture to the tops of heads," he said) but furnished us with a printed summary of each lecture. One quotation from his summary read: "Many people think great crises produce great leaders. Don't you ever believe it. History is full of crises that produced nothing but a crop of weak leaders. When you face a crisis in your life, there is only one person you can depend on to guide you through it. That person is yourself."

When I returned to Princeton for my sophomore year in the fall of 1906, I found my class deeply involved in lining up for sections, which would be taken into membership the following spring in the upper-class eating clubs. Princeton had abolished fraternities long before, but social distinctions were preserved in the eating clubs. These were all just off campus on Prospect Street. Freshmen were banned from them because they were the holy of holies. Their social status was like a flight of stairs from bottom to top. The oldest clubs—such as Ivy, Tiger Inn, and Cottage—were at the top. The newest clubs—Terrace, Key and Seal—were at the bottom.

A lot of maneuvering went on in my class to get into a high-ranking club. It kept the class in turmoil and interfered with our studies. The graduates from the eastern prep schools had help from the upperclassmen of their schools to get them into the better clubs. Most of my friends were boys from western high schools and we had an eating club of our own at Renwicks on Nassau Street known as White Hats.

The White Hats didn't rank very high socially on campus, but that didn't bother us until the start of an annual frenzy called "Bicker Week," when the various clubs began forming sections of sophomores to be invited as members. Some of the White Hats were taken into top clubs, some into lower, and some not at all. The men who didn't make a club were called "sadbirds," and they were scorned by the joiners. Some stayed out because they couldn't afford it or didn't get bids because of some peculiarity of looks, or were not sociable, or were "grinds," or did not part their hair just right. As things turned out, some of the non-joiners became the most distinguished members of our class. Several of us White Hats wanted to stay together through our junior and senior years, and I was delegated to ask the president by letter how we could manage this.

President Wilson received me graciously in his office in the tower room of '79 Hall at the head of Prospect Street. He began by asking me about myself. I told him how much I enjoyed being a summer cowboy at Dawson's Ranch in Routt County and how I was seriously considering a ranching career. He replied that easterners were inclined to underestimate the importance of the West in American life and added that one of his best friends and colleagues at Johns Hopkins was Frederick Jackson Turner, whose writings had done more than any other historian to educate people about the West.

Before discussing my eating club problem, President Wilson told me that I had come to him at a good time because of his interest in two reforms for the university, eliminating the snobbery of the club system and restoring a measure of discipline to the body of undergraduates.

To illustrate the matter of student discipline, he explained that a senior had been found keeping a girl in his room on Nassau Street and Dean Henry B. Fine had expelled him. The punishment was considered severe and the mother of the expelled student came to Wilson's office wearing widow's dress to demand a lesser penalty. The mother said that her son's father and grandfather were Princeton graduates and her son had been raised from childhood with the idea that graduating from Princeton was the big event that would launch him in his life's career.

"When the mother saw by my expression that I was not affected by this idea, she threw back the veil concealing her face and said, 'My doctors tell me that I must have major surgery to save my life. If I have that operation with the knowledge of my son's disgrace, I will not survive the surgery.' To this plea I responded, 'Madam, you put me in a difficult position, but I must uphold Dean Fine's decision.' " No more words were spoken and Dr. Wilson bowed her out the door.

I couldn't resist asking him, "Did she die?"

"No," he answered, "and her son was not readmitted either."
He added that he had felt like the old English judges when they
donned the black cap and sentenced criminals to death. Back at
home, it made him sick to his stomach, and Mrs. Wilson found
him ill in the bathroom.

As he turned now to the club matter, Dr. Wilson walked over
to the big window in his office which looked down Prospect Avenue. "Some of the wealthy New York and Pennsylvania people
with sons here would like to turn this college into a Tuxedo Institution, a country club. I refuse to head such an establishment. For
the moment I have been considering a scheme to have eligibility
to the clubs supervised by a faculty committee and not left for the
students themselves to do."

Coming to my immediate problem, he said, "If you don't join
an upper-class club you will have to eat in a commercial restaurant and you will have no place to entertain your family or
friends when they come to see you. For that reason, I can't advise
you not to join a club. But if you do, your White Hats would be
happier if you could all stay together." We took his suggestion
and we were invited as a body into Campus Club. Campus was a
middle-rated club housed in an old wooden house which had
formerly been the residence of Dean West.

As soon as my group pledged ourselves to Campus, we undertook to elevate the club's standing. The best way to do this was
to build a fine brick edifice, replacing the old wooden house. To
do this, we had to get the consent of the mortgage holders on the
old structure, which was not hard to do. I then made trips to
New York and Philadelphia to raise money for the building from
alumni. Much of my sophomore year was spent on this campaign. When it was over, the funds assured, and an architect
selected, it occurred to some of us that we were following the
pattern of club snobbery that President Wilson wanted to
change.

Again I made an appointment to see him and asked if we could
get the two clubs on each side of Campus—Terrace and
Quadrangle—to consolidate with us. We would do away with
the old buildings and operate as Dr. Wilson wished, with membership determined by lot under supervision of the university.
President Wilson told me that he liked the Quad plan but that he
personally was not in a position just then to promote it. That was

enough assurance for me. To be an agent in furthering a reform in social justice at Princeton seemed a tremendous opportunity.

I arranged for President Wilson to come for dinner at each of the three clubs concerned so that he could explain the Quad plan and show how it would eradicate the undemocratic side of the club system. The undergraduates and the alumni who heard him were enthusiastic about the plan. But the estimates of moving the old clubs and building a new large brick one exceeded our budget by $100,000.

Terrace Club had a member by the name of Ted Slocum. He was a nephew of the widow of Russell Sage, the railroad tycoon who had already given millions to Princeton. I asked Ted to ask his aunt if she would contribute $100,000 to complete our budget to build the first Quadrangle Clubhouse. Ted promised to do so during a family gathering over Easter. I went down to the Princeton railway station to meet his train.

As Ted left the train, I rushed up to him in a state of wild excitement. "Will she put up the money?" I asked.

"Yes she will," Ted said, "if President Wilson will ask her for it."

I was overwhelmed with joy at Ted's report. I felt that victory was ours for all our hard work and that Woodrow Wilson's dream of a Quadrangle to improve social life at Princeton was to be tried out. Flushed with triumph, I rushed to Prospect and rang the doorbell. President Wilson opened the door himself and I blurted out the news that Mrs. Sage would put up the $100,000 when he asked her for it. Too elated to be intelligible, I used the words of the witch in the *Rime of the Ancient Mariner* when she won the dice throw and exclaimed, "The game is done, I've won, I've won!" To my amazement, Dr. Wilson's long face hardened. He said, "I can't ask Mrs. Sage to do something the trustees do not favor."

I was stunned. The president explained that he had become president of Princeton in 1902 with the backing of wealthy men such as Moses Taylor Pyne; Cyrus McCormick, the Chicago reaper king; and his Princeton classmate, Cleveland Dodge. These powerful trustees, he said, had favored the Quad plan at first and then had turned against it, voting that the university could not afford the cost of it, that many alumni opposed it, that aristocracy was a fact of life even in democratic America, and that the plan was Utopian and in violation of previous commitments to Dean West for establishing a graduate college.

Though I asked Dr. Wilson to compromise his scruples enough to ask Mrs. Sage for the $100,000 to finance something he believed in, I realized it was useless to argue with him further. I was close to tears as I turned and walked out of Prospect into the night.

Though we had failed to get our Quad plan, our new brick Campus Club was built and ready for us by my senior year. After graduation I wrote President Wilson to say that I understood and sympathized with his decision. He replied the next day:

June 17th, 1909

My dear Mr. Carpenter:

I need not tell you how warmly I appreciate your letter of June 16th. I think that our talks together have established a delightful understanding between us with regard to the whole club situation in Princeton. I perfectly understand the purposes of the Campus Club in undertaking its new building, and I beg to assure you that nothing could be more gratifying to me than the assurances with which your letter closes. I shall certainly think of the Campus Club as one of my chief allies in pushing forward the interest of the University.

Cordially and sincerely yours,
Woodrow Wilson

I am quite certain that Woodrow Wilson's failure to get trustee approval of the Quad plan was a major tragedy of his life. It led to his resignation from Princeton, his turning to politics, his acceptancy of the candidacy to run for governor of New Jersey in 1910, and finally his election as president of the United States in 1912.

As the historian Henry Wilkinson Bragdon wrote in his book *Woodrow Wilson: The Academic Years* (Harvard University Press, 1967), "The Quad struggle embittered Wilson and brought out the harsh side of his character not before revealed but at the same time it toughened him so that he was later able to deal with politicians on their own terms. It made him distrustful of wealth and enlarged his social sympathies."

FOUR

HOMESTEADING

It was with a feeling of relief in June 1907 that I left the foggy dews of New Jersey and the turmoil of Princeton's Bicker Week to return to the peace of the mountains and breathe the high, dry, fragrant air of Colorado's Western Slope. Again I boarded Dave's stagecoach at Wolcott and heard him talk about "huggin' the schoolmarms" as the coach swayed through McCoy to Yampa. Dave told me that his stage days would end soon because David Moffat's cliff-hanging railroad from Denver had broken the isolation of Routt County by way of Gore Canyon and would reach Hayden in a few more years. From Yampa I staged two days more past Steamboat Springs and on to Hayden.

While I was away at college, my Evanston High School friend, Jack White, had taken over my board-and-room summer job at the Dawson Ranch. Jack and I had forgotten our quarrel about the Taos fiasco. Mr. Dawson found odd jobs for me on my return to Hayden. Things had not changed much, though I found that an eight-foot-high woven wire fence had been built around a pasture of the Dawson Ranch across the Yampa River. Wishing to maintain his frontier way of life, Mr. Dawson had installed in the pasture the buffalo that Mr. Goodnight had given him, along with a band of sixteen wild elk. In March, when the Rocky Mountain sheep were lambing in the Flat Top Mountains south of Hayden, Mr. Dawson got permission from the state game commission to capture two lambs, a buck, and a ewe.

Jack White went with a well-known hunter, Morris Pidcock,

into the high country to catch them. This they did by running the sheep into fresh snow, where the lambs were easily captured. Jack and Morris bottle-fed the lambs and slept in bed with them until the two men could get them out of the highlands to the ranch to complete Mr. Dawson's menagerie of Colorado wildlife. He also had a cage with two young bobcats in it. But when one of the bobcats nearly bit his thumb off, he went to the house, got his gun, and shot both of them.

One of my odd jobs for Mr. Dawson in June and July was to carry the "rear rod" for Mr. Dawson's surveyor, Charles Harkness, to locate the corners of a school section (land given to each state to finance public schools). There were two of these unfenced school sections, numbers 16 and 36, in each thirty-six-square-mile township. They were administered laxly for pasturage by the state land commissioners, and Mr. Dawson needed extra pasturage for his increasing numbers of horses and mules.

Such pasturage was getting scarce around Hayden because President Theodore Roosevelt had just withdrawn as national forest a vast acreage of the public domain. These lands had been used free of charge by ranchers for the grazing of their livestock, but like anything else that is given away free of charge, the ranchers soon overstocked the public domain with cattle and sheep, and deterioration of the land resulted. Gifford Pinchot, Roosevelt's head of the U. S. Forest Service, became alarmed over this threat to the timber resources in the high mountains. The timber held back and conserved snow water, which flowed down for agricultural use below. To protect the timberlands, Roosevelt created Routt National Forest and White River National Forest. These forests, lands that had always been wide-open free range, were subject now to federal supervision and grazing fees.

On the survey crew, we stopped one day about ten miles northwest of Hayden on a little rise of scrub oak to eat our lunch by a spring. The spot enchanted me. Morgan Creek, dry in summer, was nearby. I could see Wolf Mountain eastward and the Flat Top Mountains seventy-five miles south.

While we ate, Mr. Harkness studied his survey map and said to me, "This spring has always been considered to be on state land, and for that reason it could not be homesteaded. But the line we've just run shows that the spring is twenty-four feet south of the school section's south line and on the federal government's public domain. As soon as somebody finds that out, they'll homestead the tract that includes the spring. It's the only dependable stock water for miles in any direction, and for that reason it controls many hundreds of acres of public grazing land all around it."

Mr. Harkness's words made me feel like a man who had stumbled on a gold mine. I decided to keep my mouth shut and homestead that spring if possible. The chief drawback was that I would not be eligible to homestead until I was twenty-one years old, which would be August 10, 1907—forty days in the future. I rode back to the ranch and consulted Mr. Dawson about it. He advised me to take a camp outfit and a bed at once and establish residence at the spring, to hide it with rocks, and put a sign on it stating that it was "Farrington R. Carpenter's" homestead. He told me further to stake my horse at the spring and to water the horse there every day for the forty days before I became twenty-one, and to keep a rifle handy and be prepared to look mean if somebody else tried to file on it.

It was an anxious forty days but no one bothered me. Early on August 10, I was the first applicant when Ezekiel Shelton, the land commissioner, opened the door of the Hayden land office. I filed my claim on the 160 acres, including the spring, under the Homestead Act of 1862, and filed for an additional 160 acres adjoining it under the Desert Land Act of 1877. Title to the desert land could be obtained by irrigating twenty acres, which I planned to do by impounding the overflow of the spring into a reservoir, augmented by occasional water from Morgan Creek.

I should digress here to explain that part of my joy in that homestead filing derived from my feeling that I was playing a role in a unique historical process. The distractions of Princeton during my sophomore year had not kept me from thinking of a time when I would become a rancher and own land myself. To find out how ranchers in Routt County had gotten title to their land, and how the public domain was distributed in general, I had gone to the Princeton library to read up on two events which were as thrilling to me as the American Revolution.

One event was the passage of the Basic Land Ordinance of 1785, which divided the unclaimed public domain of the Ohio country—and the future million-square-miles of the Louisiana Purchase of 1803—into townships six miles square. Each township was divided again into thirty-six sections of 640 acres, each of which anyone could acquire for two dollars an acre (free after the Homestead Act of 1862). The second event was the enactment of the Northwest Ordinance of 1787, by which the public domain, filling up in time with land-hungry people, would become a self-governing part of the United States, first as a territory and then as a full-fledged state. I felt that this remarkable system of land distribution, in contrast to the feudal system in the rest of the world, was the keystone to the success of American democracy.

When I wrote my father about my 320-acre homestead, which I called Oak Point, I explained with special pride that I was starting manhood owning a piece of the United States half a mile square, which was larger than the entire city of Evanston, Illinois. I also told my Yankee-born father that I had become a Texan by heritage, as my homestead near Hayden lay on land that Texas had once claimed before relinquishing it as part of the Compromise of 1850.

In a few days I received a certificate from the Glenwood Springs land office stating that my application had been approved. With paper in hand, I felt that I was a frontiersman at last, a citizen of the American fraternity of empire builders—the possessor of land claimed first by the Indians, acquired by the United States, and now to be developed by a new member of the "Do-it-yourself-or-it-won't-get-done" club.

The land office sent me a pamphlet, *Requirements for Homesteaders*. I discussed its contents with old-timers in Hayden, and it became my favorite reading. One paragraph read: "A habitable residence must be established within six months of the date of filing the claim, and some cultivation of the land must be made in the six months period." The old-timers explained that this cultivation rule was met by buying a package of turnip seed and scattering it around to produce what was called "a homesteader's acre" of planting.

After establishing residence on his homestead, the entryman had to "maintain residence" there seven out of twelve months yearly for five consecutive years. To "prove up" on a claim after the five years, three neighbors had to testify to the homesteader's compliance with the requirements. This was easy to get, as the popular sentiment was, "If you will testify for me, I will testify for you." Hayden residents were eager to get the nontaxable public domain on the tax rolls so that the homesteader would help pay for roads and schools.

The land office sent inspectors to check on the homesteader's compliance. All kinds of dodges were used to fool them—such as carrying ashes from a friend's ranch to make the homestead look inhabited.

Since I had to be back in Princeton in September for my junior year, I had less than a month to make a homesteader out of myself. My first job was to get food and cook my own meals. My nearest neighbors were Mr. and Mrs. George L. Murphy, who had a small ranch on the Dry Fork of Elkhead Creek, two and a half miles from my claim. They were an elderly, hospitable couple who were pleased to have a near neighbor. They kept a milk cow and poultry yard as well as a pigpen, and they offered to sell me eggs and milk. They recommended that I go to Fred Schaefermeyer, a bachelor who lived three miles south of my claim, for help in building a cabin.

Mr. Schaefermeyer was of Danish descent. He had wandered into Routt County in the 1890s from the booming gold camp at Cripple Creek, Colorado, and had homesteaded a ranch at the foot of Wolf Mountain, making ends meet by opening a blacksmith shop in Hayden. In the course of time he had twenty acres of cropland, a team of horses, wagon and buckboard, farm machinery, potato cellar, a milk cow, sheep, hogs, and a lot of chickens. He was considered a well-to-do "batch homesteader" and was noted for his skill with a broadaxe. Living alone as he did, Fred had very positive ideas about how things should be done. He was a perfectionist.

When I rode over to Fred Schaefermeyer's ranch, I found him busy stacking hay. He told me that he couldn't help me cut down forty logs to use as a frame (he called it the "pen") for my cabin until he got his hay up. I offered to help with the hay, and next day I showed up bright and early at his place. I helped him hay for four days. Being troubled with hay fever, I had to stuff my nostrils full of bits of red bandana and breathe through my mouth to be able to handle the dusty hay without sneezing all the time.

After the haying, Fred took me into the Wolf Mountain timber and showed me how to select trees that would make good eighteen- to twenty-foot house logs and how to fell them so that they would fall where they could be easily skidded out for loading. Before he chopped down a tree, he would plant a stake where he wanted it to fall and in nearly all cases it would fall on the stake and drive it into the ground.

I borrowed a team of mares and the running gears of a wagon from Mr. Dawson and learned how to load the logs on the wagon by myself. I did this by putting two poles on the front and back wheel on one side, tying my lariat rope to the wagon centerpiece, looping the rope around the log, and rolling it up by having my saddle horse pull the rope. Fred came over and showed me how to place flat rocks for the corner foundations of my cabin while he notched and saddled the corner ends of two logs and fitted them together. Fred was a proud craftsman. "When I notch and saddle two logs to fit," he told me, "you can't put a toothpick in the notch."

The space between the logs was chinked with wood and filled with daubing of lime and cement on the outside. Fred said that the daubing would stay on better if it had hair mixed in it. So I got a bag full of hair sweepings from the barber in Hayden and mixed them in the daub. All of one side of the cabin had red hair in the daub from one old red-headed settler who had a yearly hair trim.

Using his broadaxe, Fred planed off the inside of each log as we piled them up so that the cabin had a flat internal face. When the pen of the twelve- by eighteen-foot cabin was completed ten logs high, I nailed on boards to keep the logs in place after sawing in openings for doors and two windows. The chips and extra pieces were used on the inside to stop up the openings between logs. On the outside I chinked in a combination of cement, lime, and sand. After Fred left to go back to his ranch work, I got a neighbor to haul out lumber from Hayden for a roof.

None of my neighbors approved of where I had placed the cabin. At Oak Point I had a view of Cedar Mountain beyond the town of Craig and the sage prairies westward, with the Flat Tops to the south. They thought I should have placed it in the gulch by the spring so I wouldn't have to carry water so far. Nor did they approve of my gently sloping roof, saying it would break down with the heavy winter snows unless I brought it to a sharp peak. But it was September by now and time to head back to Princeton. I wrote the land office and was given permission to leave my homestead "for purposes of education."

Since my new home was habitable, I quit my summer tent and spent the last few nights inside the cabin. Following Fred's instructions, I skinned the hide off the hoof end of the front leg of an elk, a deer, and a Rocky Mountain sheep, and made three coat hooks of them to give a Routt County atmosphere to my Princeton living room in Brown Dormitory. For still more range flavor, I took back to Princeton a side of bacon, an iron skillet, and some sagebrush. The sagebrush soon expired in the humid New Jersey atmosphere.

When I finished my junior year at Princeton and returned to Hayden in June 1908, I brought my old friend, Jack White, with me. When we reached my claim, we found to my surprise that Fred Schaefermeyer had come over to Oak Point with a team, a plow, and harrow and had plowed out an irrigation ditch from the spring to a patch of open land below it, back of my cabin—all without request or pay from me. The radishes and lettuce that he had planted were already up in my irrigated garden.

Jack was a year younger than I but would become twenty-one years old that summer. He filed on a homestead and a desert land claim on Morgan Creek between the Schaefermeyer homestead and Oak Point. We planned to work together and fence our joint 640-acre claims and eventually go into the cattle business. Jack built a dam in Morgan Creek which would enable us in time to store water in the spring runoff, when the creek went dry in July.

The matter of getting fence posts for several miles of barbed-wire fence to hold our horses and milk cow was important. We could get quaking aspen fence posts for the taking, but they rotted at the ground level in a year or two. Cedar fence posts were the best, but there were no cedar trees near us. Fred said if quaking aspen trees were cut during a thirty-day period in the fall, when sap was neither going up to the branches nor down to the roots, the posts would not rot. We contracted with Fred to cut several hundred quaking aspen posts at that particular time of year. They never did rot, and some of them could be found standing after thirty years' use.

Through that summer Jack and I had plenty of vegetables from the garden Fred had put in for us. We ate a lot of grouse and sage chicken—then still, though their numbers were declining, a delicious specialty of the Routt County homesteaders. I built a second room to my cabin and a second story and cut timber for a log barn and corral which I planned to put up the following summer.

During that summer Jack and I agreed that the time had come for us to go into the cattle business and make practical use of our two homesteads. We had buildings, saddle horses, corrals, lariats, and snubbing posts, which were all that was needed then to handle the cattle. The branch of the business that we liked was the raising of purebred Hereford bulls for local sale.

Routt County was in what was called Round Up District No. 25, where we could graze our cattle free of charge under the supervision of three commissioners named by the state governor. Owners of cows on this District No. 25 public domain—or "Range" as it was known locally—were required to furnish a bull of eighteen months of age for every twenty-five head of cows on the range. Only bulls of purebred Shorthorn or Hereford lineage were allowed on the range. A custom had been established of using Shorthorn bulls for three consecutive years and then alternating with Hereford bulls for the next three years. Such rotation was calculated to produce the best calves.

There were already two raisers of purebred Shorthorn bulls in our district and no local breeders of purebred Hereford bulls. To Jack and me this seemed a golden opportunity to raise Hereford bulls for our range. However, the first thing we needed was capital.

Passing through Chicago on the way east for my last year at Princeton, I asked my father for a loan of $2,500 to fund the partnership of Carpenter and White. My father's shoe factory in Holland, Michigan, was doing well. He favored our venture and loaned us the money at no interest if we would give him one third of our net profits. He predicted that there would be no profit for the first few years but that the herd would increase and there would be profit for all of us in time. Of course, Father approved of Jack White as my partner, having admired Jack's initiative in earning his keep since he was twelve years old.

At the same time, my father told me that I had the makings of a lawyer and that he would put me through law school if I were so inclined. During the winter I applied for admittance to Harvard Law School and was accepted. Meanwhile, Jack spent my father's loan, buying twenty-five purebred Hereford cattle at one hundred dollars a head at the dispersal sale of the Elias Ammons

RIGHT: *Beau Blanchard 64th was very gentle but served a far better purpose than to carry Hayden's youngsters around (about 1919).* CENTER: *Jack White (front) and Ferry Carpenter in buckboard with camping outfit, 1908.* BOTTOM: *Original homestead cabin at Oak Point built by Fred Schaefermeyer and Farrington Carpenter. Standing in front of the cabin are Carpenter (right) and Billy Flannery.*

herd at Parshall, Colorado, in Middle Park. In the spring he trailed them to our Routt County homesteads.

The cows we bought were identified by tattoos in their ears, and each had a certificate of registration in the American Hereford Association with offices in Kansas City, Missouri. The certificate gave the name, number, birth date, and two generations of pedigree of the animal, as well as the name of its breeder. The cows themselves were no different from ordinary commercial cattle except that the recording of their ancestry gave an assurance of similarity in color and markings of their progeny to the standard pattern of their breed. We joined the American Hereford Association under the name of Carpenter and White and began registering our calves at a fee of twenty-five cents each. The fee was soon raised to fifty cents and then to a dollar.

After graduation from Princeton in June 1909, I returned to the Carpenter and White Ranch and found that the cows had calved and we were well launched in our new business. It was customary to sell bull calves at fourteen months of age but since we had no place to keep them that long we put them up for sale at seventy-five dollars each as soon as they were weaned at eight months of age. We sold most of them but were left with a small bunch of less-desirable bulls—those with too much white hair on their backs ("linebacks") or too little on their shoulders ("red necks"). These bulls we drove to the Ute Indian Reservation in Utah one hundred miles west of Hayden. Since the Utes liked calico ponies and didn't object to off-colored bulls, we found them easy to sell.

But everywhere else we went to sell bulls we were confronted with two criticisms of the Hereford breed: they were said to be "pinchy assed," didn't have large rear quarters like the Shorthorn cattle, and the cows were inferior in milk production. To correct these deficiencies, American breeders imported Hereford bulls from the British Isles, where the breed had originated. John E. Painter, a prominent Colorado Hereford breeder, told me that a famous bull named Repeater had done much to put heavy rear quarters on Herefords. Painter said that the English breeders Gudgel and Simpson had gotten the idea of Repeater when they were in Liverpool watching the docking of a ship. A lot of Scandinavian girls returning from domestic service in the United States were leaning over the rail and waving to their friends on shore. Watching them from above, Gudgel said to Simpson, "If we can find a Hereford bull with rear quarters like those girls, we will have what is needed to improve Herefords in America."

The most difficult task in running purebred cattle on an open range, where other people's cattle also ran, was the necessity of seeing to it that our cows were bred to our own registered pure-bred Hereford bulls. If their calves showed evidence of a sire of another breed, it would be impossible to sell them for breeding purposes.

There was a big, red Shorthorn bull that belonged to a Dutchman who lived on the Yampa River. This bull took a great liking to our cows and constantly visited them. Being older and heavier than our young Hereford bull, the Shorthorn managed to do most of the honors. We saw that we could never succeed as Hereford bull producers if our calves showed Shorthorn color and markings, and we appealed to its owner to keep him home. He replied that his cattle had as good a right on public lands as ours had, and refused to cooperate. Again and again we ran the Shorthorn bull back to the Yampa, using barbed-wire quirts, but to no avail. He was always with our cows the next day.

Once, when Jack and I came home from building fence, we found that Shorthorn with our cows. There was no one in sight. We got down our ropes and stretched him out on the ground. As I was getting out my knife to castrate him, Jack had a novel idea. His mother in Evanston had sent him some hardware to be used in his new cabin—hinges, locks, and some glass doorknobs. Why not sew two glass doorknobs in the scrotum after removing the bull's testicles? That we did, and the bull went straight home when we let him up, with the new additions swinging. The owner never found out why his bull stayed home after that, al-though he strongly suspected that we had something to do with it. In town a few weeks later, he shook his buggy whip at me and said, "You boys, you think you can scare me, shust go ahead, I stay mit."

In the fall, I had to go east to Harvard Law School and Jack had all the work with the cattle to do by himself. Since we needed hay to carry the cattle through the five winter months of snow, I went to the bank to borrow money to buy it. But the local banker would not loan us money when we refused to give him a mortgage on the cattle as security for the loan. However, a cattle trader by the name of Dave Sellers, who owned a butcher shop in town, overheard my conversation with the banker and stopped me on the street. He said he would loan us money to buy hay on which to winter our cattle if we didn't pay more than six dollars a ton for it, and he wouldn't require a mortgage on the cattle.

I hastened to Reece Horton's ranch, where there was just the right amount of hay we needed. I bought it, gave him a check for it, and then rode straight to town to borrow the money and cover the check. After being assured that I had gotten a good measurement on the hay stacks, and that the price was six dollars a ton, Dave filled out a printed form of note for me to sign, but he scratched out the 8 percent interest charge and wrote in 12 percent.

"Oh, Dave," I said, "we didn't expect to have to pay more than 8 percent interest." Dave wheeled his chair so he could face me, and said, "I want to tell you something. I've been watching you boys and the way you look after your cattle, and I believe you're going to make a go of it. When I first came to this country and went into the cattle business, I had to pay 18 percent interest on money I borrowed. Now when you have to pay that kind of interest, you have to get up early in the morning and work hard all day. That 18 percent interest was the making of me. I want to help you boys succeed and that's why I'm charging you 12 percent interest." I signed the note without further protest.

FIVE

Hayden's First Lawyer

When I landed in Cambridge in the fall of 1909 and entered Harvard Law School, I found an entirely different kind of life from the happy-go-lucky years I had known as a Princeton undergraduate. At Harvard, I learned, you did just one thing. You read law books and you went to classes. The study absorbed your life. The lecture and textbook method of instruction was sometimes referred to as the "pump and reservoir" method in which the instructor was the pump and the student the reservoir.

I spent my summers in 1910 and 1911 far from Cambridge working on my Colorado homestead at Oak Point. Since I was going to be a lawyer, I kept my eye on how the law was working around Hayden. A criminal case that was arousing great local interest in 1910 was being tried at Hahn's Peak. Having decided to attend the trial, I took my bedroll and joined a group of jurors who had been summoned. At that time Hahn's Peak was just about finished as Routt's county seat, which was moved to Steamboat Springs in 1912. Only one hotel remained at Hahn's Peak. One of its five bedrooms was reserved for the owner, another for the judge, and a third for the district attorney and court reporter. With only one room left, the jurors and witnesses brought their own camp outfits and set up tents along Willow Creek. They did not mind camping as they considered jury duty a vacation from ranch work, and the five-dollar-a-day pay was attractive.

The defendant in the case was a well-known and respected

rancher by the name of Matt Gates. He had been charged with shooting three sage chickens out of season on his ranch. I was drawn to the matter because Jack White and I had subsisted for weeks on these magnificent "cocks of the plains," or "sagehens" as they were called by ornithologists. They were the largest of all such fowl except the wild turkey, and they made superb eating— which was why they were becoming rare even in the isolation of Routt County. Their dramatic mating performance in huge flocks, where the air sacs of the males inflated to produce a great racket, made them one of the most remarkable fowls in the world.

The prosecution witness was a newcomer named Hobson who had run for county clerk and recorder in the preceding year against the popular incumbent, John Crawford. Stung by defeat at the polls, Hobson vowed to get even with the voters, whom he called "the biggest bunch of liars in the state of Colorado." To get revenge, Hobson had himself appointed humane officer with the power of arrest and enforcement of the game laws, which were never strictly observed in our newly settled district.

Soon after his appointment, as he was driving up Deep Creek one day, Hobson saw Gates unhitch his team from a mower and start toward the house for dinner. Gates carried a .22 caliber rifle, and on the way to the house, he shot and killed three sage chickens. Humane Officer Hobson met him as he reached the house, placed him under arrest for violation of the game laws, and ordered him bound over to the district court in Hahn's Peak.

Word of this arrest spread like wildfire and aroused great indignation all over the county. Many of the inhabitants felt they had a constitutional right to shoot sage chickens on their own land at any time for their own needs. A committee of the most prominent citizens in Hayden went to Meeker and tried to persuade James C. Gentry, the district attorney, to dismiss the case. When Gentry refused, they returned to Hahn's Peak predicting that he would be overwhelmingly defeated at the next election.

When the case was called in the log courthouse at Hahn's Peak, the room was crowded with concerned people. Hobson took the stand, and prosecutor Gentry asked him to describe what he had seen the accused do. At the end of the testimony, Gentry asked, "Are you sure it was sage chickens that were killed?"

"Yes," Hobson answered. "I took possession of the sagehens and left them in a gunnysack in the vault of the courthouse. They are with me today."

"Show them to the jury," Gentry said. Thereupon Hobson emptied his sack, and out fell three dead owls. Turning plaintively to the judge, Hobson said, "Your Honor, someone has switched birds on me."

The judge dismissed the case, and Hobson was never seen again in Routt County. At the next election, Gentry was reelected district attorney by an almost unanimous vote.

In June 1912, after my graduation from Harvard Law School, I took the Colorado bar exams in Denver. After passing them, I returned to Hayden—this time via the Moffat Railroad to Steamboat Springs.

Now, having followed my father's wishes, I was a lawyer. Along with my Oak Point homestead, I owned a small herd of cattle with Jack White and had a few good saddle horses. In love with the ranching business, I had no particular interest in practicing law, but my father had spent a good deal of money sending me through law school. To set up a practice, I would need to have an office in Hayden since this was the only town near Oak Point. Hayden had never had a lawyer and, to my mind, did not need one—but I decided to *make* it need one.

Hayden was a little bit of a town in 1912, not even a county seat. I nevertheless regarded its setting in the fertile valley of the Yampa River as one of the most beautiful spots on earth—and I continued to think so all my life. Hayden had 410 inhabitants, two hotels, three livery stables, three blacksmith shops, a newspaper, a barber shop, general stores, surveyors' offices, and saloons. It also had a schoolhouse, a church, a drugstore, two banks, and a saddle shop. Its one physician, Dr. Solandt, doubled as a veterinarian. When Hayden was incorporated in 1906, it acquired a justice of the peace and a constable. I asked an old-timer if Hayden had grown much in the last ten years, and he said he didn't think so. The population, he said, was constant because he noticed that quite often when a new baby was born, some man left town.

My first requirement in establishing myself as a lawyer was to find a proper law office. I rented a lean-to beside one of the town's two banks. The lean-to, which had originally been a one-lane bowling alley, was eight feet wide and thirty-two feet long and had not been occupied for years. I was to pay ten dollars a month rental, which included the use of the bank's outhouse, and I had to make my own repairs on the building. I got the help of Alvin D. Galloway, a neighboring homesteader and a carpenter by trade. When I asked him to construct a partition inside so that I could have an outer office and a back bedroom, Al considered the extra wall useless. After I explained the need for an attorney to have confidential relations with his clients, he finally got the point—and expressed his understanding of it by saying, "I see, you're going to bleed 'em up here, and breed 'em back there."

After I hung out my shingle, I displayed my certificate of admission to the bar and my diplomas. I borrowed an extra typewriter from the bank and bought a 1908 copy of the Colorado statutes. Business was slow coming. I had plenty of inquisitive callers and people who wanted to discuss local politics, but few clients.

To help me out, both banks promised that if I would take out a commission as a notary public, they would send me those customers who needed to have their signatures notarized on chattel mortgages or trust deeds to secure loans. For this I received twenty-five cents per chattel mortgage and one dollar per deed of trust. I hung up my certificate as a notary public, which was issued under the hand of the secretary of state and garnished with the great seal of the state of Colorado as well as a large orange ribbon. The certificate seemed to impress the public more than either of my fancy Princeton and Harvard diplomas.

One day A. P. Wood, the manager of one of Hayden's stores, rushed into my office. "Ferry," he said, "I've got a big case for you." He explained that Old Man Wingrove, a Mormon who had once lived in Hayden and raised vegetables for sale, had moved to Vernal, Utah, two years previously. He had rented his house to W. S. Price, the justice of the peace, but except for the first month had never received his ten-dollar-a-month rental. Having read in the local paper that Hayden now had a lawyer, he wanted to collect the two years' back rental or evict Judge Price.

I was not overjoyed at assuming in my first case the task of evicting a justice of the peace before whom I would have to practice. However, I decided to take the risk. To keep things on as friendly a basis as possible, I went to Judge Price's place to tell him what I had been employed to do. He was there when I called, and his wife, a seamstress, was busy at her sewing machine in the living room while two children played on the floor.

When I explained my mission to the judge, he was surprised and indignant. "Did Mr. Wingrove tell you what he owes *me*?" he exclaimed. "When it's all figured out, he'll owe *me* more than *I* owe *him*! I'll let my wife tell you about the condition of this house when we first moved in." Mrs. Price, who had stopped her sewing and was listening intently, said, "Oh, Mr. Carpenter, when we moved in here, there were so many bedbugs they were sifting down from the ceiling. We couldn't sleep here until they were all cleaned out."

The judge, seeing that I was now on the defensive, continued to bristle. "And that's not all," he said. "Come with me." He took me into the kitchen and through a door into an adjoining shed. Pointing out a window toward the outhouse, he said, "The people who lived here before us were so damn lazy they wouldn't shovel a path to the outhouse in the winter. They just lifted up a plank here and used *this* for their outhouse. We had to clean it all out. What do you think *that's* worth?"

I had taken a course in damages at Harvard under Professor Waumbaugh, who was an authority on the subject, but I could remember nothing in his lectures that would apply to this situation. I also knew that the whole town was aware of the defaulted rent and of my undertaking to collect it.

When we got back into the living room, I said, "Judge, how would it be if Mr. Wingrove canceled one year's back rent for your cleaning the house of bedbugs, and the other year for cleaning out the back shed? Then you can start paying rent at the end of this month."

"That would be satisfactory," he replied.

On the first day of the month, I went to the secondhand shop the judge ran and greated him with a cheery "First of the month, Judge."

"Yes, I know it is," he answered, "and I have a big draft coming in this Saturday for some coyote hides I shipped two weeks ago. Come back then, and I'll pay you."

I knew I would be foiled again if I left his shop without that month's rent. Not knowing exactly what course to pursue, I suddenly spied a .22 caliber rifle on the counter. I owned a 30-30 but it was too big for shooting sage chickens, and I needed a smaller-caliber gun.

"Is that for sale?" I asked. When he said it was, I asked the price, and he said it was ten dollars. "How would it be, Judge, if I took the .22 for the month's rent due today?"

"That'll be satisfactory, if you'll give me a receipt for this month and also for the two years' back rent," he replied.

He prepared the receipt; I signed it and took the rifle back to my office in triumph. Then I wrote to Mr. Wingrove, told him of my success, and enclosed my check for eight dollars, which was for one month's rent less my commission of two dollars.

After office hours I went to the livery barn to get my horse and ride home. Since I had no gun scabbard, I had to tie the gun under the stirrup fender. While I was doing that, Hiram Fisk, a pioneer ranchman who was standing nearby, said, "Let me see that gun." I handed to him.

"This is mine," he said. "I left it with Judge Price for repairs. Looks like it's fixed now." And he walked away with it.

Judge Price now had a receipt for two years' and one month's rent, Mr. Wingrove would soon have eight dollars of my money, Mr. Fisk had his gun back, and I had gained some experience in the perils of collecting.

In later years, I found that Judge Price performed the duties of his office as justice of the peace in an able manner. Most of the cases brought before him were for violation of the town's ordinances, which forbade bronc riding on the main street, turning milk cows loose in the town, and keeping roosters there that crowed too early in the morning. The judge's one weakness seemed to be an unwillingness to meet current bills. Around town he was known as C.O.D. Price, as all his purchases came to him by mail marked Cash on Delivery.

When I told my hard-luck story to Alva Jones, the owner of a livery stable, he went a long way toward restoring my self-confidence. He told me that he had some overdue and unpaid promissory notes that he would give me to collect, and I could keep half of what I got for my fee. Once a year, he said, a Nebraska owner of a Percheron stallion came to town with his horse and bred the mares of local ranchers for a fee. This was usually paid with a promissory note, some of which Jones, as liveryman, would buy at a discount to pay for the feed and rent that he had furnished to the stallion as well as room and board for its owner.

I took on the case and wrote to every one of the defaulting ranchers threatening them with a lawsuit if they failed to pay their notes, including a penalty for default. I didn't have long to wait for a response. Charley Cozzens, one of the best horse raisers in the community, was banging on the door of my office before I was out of bed the next day. When I let him in, he shouted, "What do you mean billing me for a twenty-five-dollar service when I only owe five?" It seemed the scale of fees for the stallion was twenty-five dollars for a service guaranteeing a foal that would stand and suck, fifteen dollars for one service and no guarantee of a foal, and five dollars for one leap. All he bargained for was one leap, Charley said, and that was all he was going to pay for. Accordingly, all the other debtors swore they had only agreed to pay five dollars for one leap, and the result was neither profitable nor satisfactory either to Jones or myself. My career as a bill collector took another tumble.

At the time I arrived in Hayden, the townsfolk were talking about large deposits of coal that Ferdinand V. Hayden, in his 1877 *Atlas of Colorado*, had reported in Routt County. There was, however, no coal mining in the county except in what were called "wagon mines," and the coal from these was sold to local ranchers. When the market for coal increased, more small outcrop mines—called "gopher hole" mines because the operators did not tunnel far underground—were opened up. They escaped examination by the state mine inspector and could be worked without conforming to state regulations.

One of these "gopher hole" coal mines was at Bear River, a small town seven miles from Hayden. One day a group of coal miners from Bear River came to my office and asked me to collect their unpaid wages. They all had notebooks showing the dates and hours of their labor. The single most difficulty in starting a suit to collect was the fact that the only name by which they knew their employer was "Joe." They knew neither his last name nor his Denver address. After they had mined and loaded three railroad cars full of coal, he had shipped the cars to Denver and disappeared. Inquiring about Joe's assets, I learned that all he had was a shed containing sacks of cement to be used in constructing a portal for the mine. The reports revealed, however, that the cement was worth several hundred dollars. It was a typical *in rem* action against the property. The plaintiffs petitioned the court to seize the defendant's assets and hold them in

TOP: *Phil Wilson and "Skinny" Carpenter as first-year law students on Boston Commons, 1909.* BOTTOM: *Hayden's first lawyer, Farrington Carpenter, with James H. Whetstone, for whom Carpenter won his first full-fledged litigation over a right of way for the Moffat Road.*

RIGHT: *Farrington Carpenter and Lee Barnes with wolf hides taken from Wolf Mountain and Pilot Knob, about 1915.* BOTTOM: *Railroad Day in Hayden, 1913.*

its jurisdiction until their claim could be adjudicated. By consulting Allen's *Colorado Justice Manual*, I found that this could be done by a constable from the justice of the peace's court. Judge Price had no regularly elected constable, but the law allowed him, in such cases, to appoint a special constable who would exercise all the powers of a regular one.

Judge Price appointed Fred Lilly, a well-known town loafer who owed him money, as special constable and sent him to Bear River to take possession of the shed of cement and to post a notice of the action on the door. The case had aroused popular interest, and I congratulated myself on my role as a champion of labor.

The defendant did not arrive from Denver, and it looked as though the outcome would be a default judgment. However, on the day of the hearing, thirty minutes before the proceedings were to begin, a livery rig from Steamboat Springs arrived bearing retired Judge Gooding, the "Nester" of the Routt County Bar. I liked Judge Gooding, for he had been friendly to me, and I pitied him because he was in a case he had no chance of winning.

The court was crowded. I put all my witnesses on the stand, and they recited their claims with no cross-examination from Judge Gooding. When I finished my presentation, he walked to the podium and asked to see the appointment of the special constable. He noted that while it had been signed by the justice of the peace, no seal had been added to his signature. Judge Gooding then read from the case of *Bruce v. Endicott*, decided on September 10, 1901, which stated that the document appointing a special constable must have a seal appended after the justice's signature. Since no seal had been appended after Justice Price's signature on Fred Lilly's appointment, the attachment of the cement was unwarranted and illegal.

When Judge Price admitted this failure, Judge Gooding asked that the case be dismissed, and announced that his client, Joe, had authorized him to take action against all who had participated in the illegal seizure of the cement. He said that while driving to Hayden that morning he had stopped at Bear River and noticed that the cement shed was leaking badly. Recent rains had saturated the sacks and turned all the cement to stone. He remarked that all parties who had a hand in the illegal seizure of the cement would be liable for damages that had occurred.

The leader of the miners' group came to the counsel table where I sat and asked me what was transpiring. All I could say was that we had come into court as plaintiffs and would soon be leaving as defendants. Fortunately, however, Joe never pressed his claim. The experience severely shook my acceptance of the idea that the common law was mankind's nearest approach to justice.

The income from my law office in the bowling alley averaged $125 a month, of which more than half came from notary public fees for work referred to me by bank cashiers to whom I gave free advice on questions that arose almost daily. The balance of my income was from the preparation of contracts, wills, and affidavits required by the General Land Office in Washington in compliance with homestead regulations. My living expenses, however, were small.

In town I purchased meal tickets at both hotels. These were good for twenty-two punches, and the cost of the ticket was only $5.50. At first I rode my horse ten miles from Oak Point to town. Later, to save paying fifty cents to keep the horse in the livery barn, I bought a bicycle and rode it until the snows came. Then, when I began spending most of my wintertime in Hayden, my office soon became a favorite loafing place for visiting ranchmen whose wives traded eggs and cream for groceries at the stores.

What I needed most was a year-round client. After long discussions with the town council, I was appointed town attorney at fifteen dollars a month. Wasting no time, I bought a rubber stamp bearing my name and title to add to my official Hayden stationery. I also compiled all the town ordinances into a booklet and had them certified under the town seal to attest that they were town law. The most monotonous part of being town attorney was staying through all the council meetings, which generally lasted until midnight and were mainly concerned with the price of hay and oats or which farmer grew the biggest potatoes.

Most of my law office practice concerned squabbles over water rights or relations between homesteaders and the General Land Office. I had little to do in domestic relations because the wives in Hayden were as anxious to preserve the status quo as their husbands. Among the settlers was George Haver, a serious man who wanted to make a go of his claim. He built a cabin and started cultivating, and his wife, a good worker, stayed right beside him and ran a good house. She kept hens and sold the eggs to the neighbors.

Each Christmas Haver would come in to see me because I had done legal work for him in getting his claim started. I would ask him about his wife, and he would say, "She's out there at the homestead and she's got to milk a cow and we're trying to get a start, and we haven't got time for her to come into town."

One Christmas he drove to town in a lumber wagon, and sitting beside him was Mrs. Haver. When George left to visit with the men in the livery barn, Mrs. Haver stepped into the outer room of my office. She was on the thin side and kind of pretty, and her hair was neat. I could see she was embarrassed. I stood up.

"How do you do, Mrs. Haver," I said. "Can I do something for you?"

"Yes," she said, "I'd like to talk with you." I escorted her to my inner office and shut the door and asked her to sit down. Without a preamble she said, "I can't stay on that homestead any more and I want a divorce. Will you be my lawyer?"

"Mrs. Haver," I replied, "you've already been on that place nearly two years and it won't be more than fourteen months before you get title to the land. Then you can sell out. You can't get anything for it now."

A small hope seemed to light in her eyes. "Do you think we can sell then, when we prove the claim?"

"Yes. Your place is a pretty good one, and I think you'd get a thousand dollars for it."

She pondered that. Then she set her lips. Finally she said, "I don't know whether I can stick it out, but I'll try."

When George returned in the lumber wagon, she climbed in and they went off. It was some time before I saw her again.

Just about a year later she walked into my office, sat down, and looked at me hard.

"Mr. Carpenter," she said, "I can't stay there any longer."

"Oh, Mrs. Haver," I said, "you're all ready to prove up. Please don't quit. Wait a little longer. It'll be worthwhile for you. Why don't you just wait it out?"

"No, I can't do it."

"Now, wait, Mrs. Haver. Why can't you do it?"

"It's just too lonely," she said. "George comes to Hayden every Saturday. I never come except at Christmas time, like this year. I'm left all alone out there. I never see nobody. How do you think I can live there?"

"Lots of women do it," I said. "Stick it out. That's what we came out West for, to stick it out."

She again went back to their homestead but came back a year later. Her chin was clamped hard. She was determined.

"Mr. Carpenter, you get me a divorce or I'll run away."

"What's the trouble, Mrs. Haver?"

She began to cry. "It's the way George treats me."

"How does he treat you?" Since I intended to get married myself one day, I was curious to find out why married couples wanted to separate. She just kept crying.

"It's my hat," she said.

"Your hat!"

"You notice the hat on my head?"

"Yes, it's quite nice looking." Then she began to bawl.

I was hoping no one would come into my office just then and hear her. I said, "What's the matter with your hat, Mrs. Haver?"

She stopped crying. "Mr. Carpenter, you don't know about that hat, so I'll tell you. George went up to the timber to work, and I hadn't seen anybody for six months but him. I was tired of looking at him. He hardly ever smiles and he doesn't say much. A few neighbors came by to get eggs, and one of them was Charlie Cozzens. I knew he was going to town, and I said, 'Charlie, will you take me to town?' He took me. I had a little egg money that I had put away and when I got to town I got out of Charlie Cozzens's wagon and went right over to Jenny Brock's ladies' shop. I haven't had a hat in seven years. Mrs. Brock had a hat that just seemed to be my kind of a hat, and I bought it. And then I went out and Charlie came by and took me home.

"It was after dark when I got there. I went in the house and I put the hat on, and George came in. He wouldn't even look at me. He went right by me into the separator room. He didn't see that hat. He separated the milk and then he sat down at the table and I waited on him while he ate his dinner. And all that time I left my hat on.

"He just sat and ate. He didn't look at me. I thought to myself, he'll just have to look up sometime and see my new hat. Finally, when he was through with his victuals, he picked up the *Breeders' Gazette* and held it up in front of his face, and there he was, reading. And there I was, standing there with my new hat. I just couldn't stand it any longer. I hauled off and I slammed that magazine out of his hand and said, 'George Haver, do you see my hat?' He said, 'Where'd you get it?' and I said, 'Jenny Brock's shop.' He said, 'What did it cost?' and I said, 'Seven dollars and a half.'"

Then she began to cry again. "And do you know what he said, Mr. Carpenter? He said, 'Jee-sus Christ!' I quit. I walked out and I won't live with that man, and that's the end."

I got Mrs. Haver her divorce. Later she went to California and married Mr. Hofsteader, a widower from Hayden. I never heard whether or not Mr. Hofsteader was the sort of man who would buy her a hat and notice it.

Having wangled my year-around town attorney stipend from the Hayden Town Council, I badgered the two Hayden banks until they agreed to pay me one hundred dollars a year to handle all their minor legal matters. I was particularly anxious to help the community in the financing of homesteads. As matters stood, homesteaders could not use their homestead claims as security for a loan because their title to the land was contingent on proving up a claim. I wrote to the Department of the Interior about the problem and the officials issued a ruling allowing homesteaders to pledge their claims as security for a loan upon payment of a filing fee to the General Land Office.

Most of the homesteaders around Hayden before World War I were having a hard time of it. Our region had nothing but rolling sagebrush and oakbrush—poor pasture land six months of the year and covered with snow most of the other six. In the little valleys with their streams a family could raise hay but no grain. The technique of dry farming was not understood yet, and the land simply would not support a family.

Thus everybody was thrilled and expectant when the Moffat Railroad arrived in Hayden from Steamboat Springs in 1913. The whole town turned out to cheer the first engine, which carried nothing more than a flat car behind it. We staged a big feast for the train crew, with elk meat and quail and trout—all cooked on stoves in the middle of the main street. After the celebration, the residents of the town put up the money to build a fine, big brick railroad station.

We supposed that the railroad's coming would transform Hayden into a prosperous city almost overnight. But after it got there—and went on seventeen miles to its final terminus at Craig—we found that we were not much better off than we had been before.

The railroad, however, did bring in a flock of land-hungry homesteaders. They would arrive in a boxcar loaded with horses, cows, plows, harrows, and disks and the family furniture—all of which they had brought hopefully from hard times in Arkansas or Kansas or wherever. By the time they left the boxcar and hired a surveyor to find a free homestead, they would have spent all of the little money they had, and so were of little immediate help to our sluggish economy.

Hayden ranchers who owned property in the path of the Moffat Road had been asked to grant the railroad a right-of-way through their land. My old friend, J. B. Dawson, was among those solicited. He dictated to me a letter for the Moffat Road. It read: "I came here from New Mexico to get away from railroads and noise. Now you have surveyed a railroad in my front yard. I can't stop civilization, so if you'll give me a siding so I can load cattle, and a mail stop, I'll give you a right-of-way through my ranch."

There were two ranch owners near Hayden who refused to give any land to the railroad. One was Mrs. Robert Williams and the other was James M. Whetstone, a well-to-do cattleman. Mrs. Williams was so opposed to having a railroad right-of-way through her ranch that she chased the surveyors off with an ax and then chopped down the tripod they had abandoned in their flight. This resulted in a contempt-of-court citation, and Mrs. Williams had to employ my admired colleague of the sagehen case, James C. Gentry, to defend her. Mr. Whetstone, on the other hand, asked me to represent him in the condemnation suit for the right-of-way over his land. He said that back in his home state of Pennsylvania the railroads never gave anything to anybody, and nobody ever gave anything to them. This was my first case in the district court, and I felt I was getting into the big league.

Mr. Whetstone was one of the best cattlemen in Routt County. As the strip of his property to be condemned was in a hay meadow, I wanted to show its high productivity. I spent several weekends at the ranch learning Whetstone's techniques. He was one of the first to recognize the value of leveling land to be irrigated so as to avoid collecting too much water in one place and too little in another. Also, most hay meadows abounded with big red ant hills that collectively equaled several acres, but Mr. Whetstone's meadows had none. When an ant hill began to form, he sank a beer bottle near it with a little syrup in the bottom, and placed it so that the bottle's opening was flush with the ground. When it filled up with ants, he corked it and threw it into the Yampa River.

That summer Mr. Whetstone cut the hay off the right-of-way strip and invited the railroad engineers to measure the stack from that section so that there would be no dispute as to its productivity. When the time came for the fall term of court at Steamboat Springs, Mr. Whetstone drove me and two witnesses to Steamboat. I had never witnessed an opening of a court of unlimited jurisdiction, and it was an impressive exhibition. The courtroom was jammed with litigants, jurymen, witnesses, and everyone else in the town who wanted to see a free show.

When Judge Shumate entered the room, the bailiff ordered everyone to stand as he announced that court was in session. The first order of business was to call the criminal docket. Mr. Gentry was handed a list of the indictments. The sheriff brought a prisoner and sat beside him inside the rail.

Turning to face the accused, Mr. Gentry would say in a firm voice, "Stand up, Mr. Smith, and listen to the indictment against you. Comes now James C. Gentry, the duly elected, qualified, and acting district attorney in and for the Ninth Judicial District of the State of Colorado and doth say . . . "

He then paused while the sheriff got the accused to his feet, whereupon he recited the known facts about the crime to be punished. He did it with such clarity and confidence that it amounted to a verbal picture of the commission of the crime. When finished, he faced the abashed defendant and said, "What do you say, Mr. Smith—guilty or not guilty?" By that time, the accused was so scared that it was often necessary for his attorney to enter a plea for him. Pleas of guilty were not uncommon.

After the entire criminal docket had been called up and the cases either set for trial or for sentence, the civil docket was called. I had hoped that the Williams case would be tried before mine, so I could see how Mr. Gentry handled it, but it seemed to be an old custom of the court to put cases of *new* attorneys first. So, the Whetstone case was set as the first trial.

A jury of six freeholders was put in the jury box, qualified, and sworn in. The lawyers on both sides made opening statements about their clients' cases, and witnesses took the witness chair and told their version of the relevant facts. Before this was completed, court was adjourned for the day.

When the trial resumed the following day and the judge had at last read his instructions to the jury, each of the opposing lawyers made a final argument. The landowner had the burden of showing the value of the land to be taken and the damage its taking would cause. So I had a chance to make two pleas to the jury. I pulled out all the stops and argued vehemently about my client's subjugation to a law that allowed railroads to penalize a ranchman by taking his property. The jury retired to consider the verdict and court was again adjourned for the day.

That evening I went to the barroom of the hotel and found Mr. Gentry seated in a large armchair with a circle of lawyers and admirers around him, including the court reporter and the district court clerk. Like Shakespeare's Falstaff, wherever Mr. Gentry sat was the head of the table. He was in a most loquacious mood, and every time he cracked a joke, the court reporter, who was well into the bottle, would laugh so hard that someone had to swat him on the back to keep him from choking.

I took a seat in the rear of the circle, but when Mr. Gentry spied me, he said, "Carpenter, do you intend to be a trial lawyer?"

"Yes, Mr. Gentry," I replied, "I do."

"I watched you today in the courtroom," he continued, "and you did everything wrong."

"What was the worst thing I did?" I inquired.

"Your worst mistake, which was the most unpardonable thing, was the way you talked to the jury in your closing argument. You must have imagined you were making a Fourth of July address in a big amphitheater the way you walked up and down in front of the jury and presented your case."

"How should I have done it?" I asked.

"Well," said Mr. Gentry, "you must first realize that men are not convinced by speeches or orations. Their minds remain susceptible to conviction only when an argument is presented to

them in a conversational tone. They like to be addressed personally and not as a member of some body. When you hunt ducks,
you don't aim at the whole flock. You pick out one bird and aim
at him. When the time comes to present your case to the jury,
you should select one member and look only at him as though
you consider him the most influential person on the jury and
very likely to be chosen as the foreman during deliberations. In a
conversational tone of voice, start talking to him until you are
sure he understands the point of view you are presenting and is
persuaded; then go on to the next juror and persuade him in the
same way."

"How do you tell when the juryman has accepted your analy-
sis of the case?" I interrupted.

"Oh, that's easy," said Mr. Gentry. "When a man gets interested in something he is listening to, his neck begins to stretch as
you grip his attention. When his Adam's apple comes out so far
that it finally chins itself on his collar, you know you have him.

"Thank God," he added, "we don't have women jurors in Colorado because they never react that way. They are always so
conscious of how their back hair may be looking that they never
allow their necks to stretch and therefore can't be totally swayed
by oratory."

The next morning the jury returned a verdict giving Mr. Whetstone one hundred dollars an acre for the four acres in the right-
of-way and one thousand dollars for the damage that resulted to
the operation of his ranch with a fenced right-of-way in the
middle of his meadow. I was relieved to learn that Mr. Whetstone was satisfied with the award.

I spent all that day watching Mr. Gentry as he set forth his client's damages from the right-of-way, and especially the
masterful way in which he wooed the jurymen, one after another, and had them giving him their intense attention. However,
the Williams jury all knew what mine in the Whetstone case had
found to be the value of the land and the damages, and they
awarded a similar amount. I always wondered what my verdict
might have been had Mr. Gentry's case been tried first.

SIX

Corralling the "She-Stuff"

Deeply involved with Hayden affairs by 1915, I suffered from a feeling that sooner or later I must terminate my carefree bachelor state and get married. When I was a child my mother had imbued me with Evanston township's ideas about matrimony—make a living, get a home, get a wife, and produce a baby. To reverse the formula was unmentionable.

Yes, I had plenty of girls. One that I admired in 1915 was a big, buxom Swiss-German teenager named Annie Elmer who lived on Morgan Bottom near my own Oak Point. Annie had only an eighth-grade education, and when her father died she took over all the work of the homestead, both the cattle raising and the farming. She was known as the best hay flanker in Routt County, and she weighed half again as much as I. At many a do-si-do quadrille, I didn't swing Annie—she swung me.

I recall a square dance at Oak Point with couples coming in rigs and on horseback from twenty miles away. Two big bonfires lighted the way past my ditches to the cabin. The indispensable Mrs. George Murphy handled the sandwiches. The bonfires heated the coffee. The dancing went on all night until 6:30 A.M. Reese Horton entertained with clogging. Bruce Dawson sang Mexican songs. Grace Peck gave us her popular recitation "Postponed Honeymoon." The caller, Sam Lighthizer, cleared the floor for Annie and me to do a waltz, just the two of us. The fiddler and banjo player took off at such a fast tempo that I was limp in ten minutes. But not Annie. She picked me up as though

I were a sack of oats and spun me around with my boots dangling while the audience cheered and hooted.

A year later, when Annie decided to become a trained nurse without the required high school diploma, I helped her get accepted for nurses' training at Jim Bardin Hospital in California. She got a free ride to California with a carload of Old Man Dawson's mules on the D&RG west from Wolcott. Later I asked her how she managed at night in the men's caboose. "I just put on overalls," she said, "piled my hair on top of my head, and tacked a muslin curtain over one bunk. I told the train crew, 'Boys, that's my bunk. Keep out.' They did."

The defection of Annie Elmer to California was a sad day for Elkhead and Morgan Bottom. North of the Yampa River, the Elkhead area had been settled almost exclusively by bachelors. Lee Barnes had a claim on Dry Fork and made his living trapping wolves for the cattle association, which paid him a bounty of fifteen dollars a wolf. Ed Knowles in California Park lived on his Spanish-American war pension. Charles, Edgar, and Clifford Fulton had homesteads on Upper Dry Fork at Elkhead. The Lighthizers from Kansas were on Lower Dry Fork. These cowboys missed Annie not only for her help with the haying but because she was the sole "she-stuff" for miles around (Mrs. Murphy was happily married). The Murphys were very hospitable and we bachelors liked to gather on Saturday evenings at the Murphy Ranch on Dry Fork to feast on Mrs. Murphy's hot soda biscuits and "woman's bread"—a welcome change from our sourdough fare.

During these evenings we discussed local affairs. A favorite topic was the scarcity of single girls in the Elkhead district. As Jack White put it, "The city slickers get away with all the 'she-stuff' that comes to Hayden, and we never even get a chance to meet them." The town boys would hear by phone of a new teacher's or telephone operator's impending arrival at Wolcott and would meet the train and propose to the girl during her three-day stage ride to Hayden.

As a law-school graduate, I was asked to solve the problem. I proposed that we get up a petition to form a new Elkhead school district by cutting off the Hayden district's north end. This section contained undeveloped anthracite coal fields, which were owned by outside capitalists. They would provide a generous share of the tax money that would build and maintain our school. The plan met with unanimous approval from the bachelors. I was elected to prepare the papers and present them to Mrs. Emma H. Peck, the county superintendent of schools, who had authority to call for elections to create new school districts.

When I presented our petition to Mrs. Peck, she got out a 1908 volume of the Colorado statutes and let me read a section stating that no new school districts could be organized out of old ones unless the new district contained ten or more children of school age. That requirement took the wind out of our sails for months.

Nevertheless, as I have mentioned, when the Moffat Railroad reached Hayden in 1913 it brought a flock of land-seekers in search of 160-acre homesteads. Jack White and the other bachelors who had filed in the Elkhead area were extremely reluctant to let new entrymen in to fence the open range and include in their land the water holes needed for our cattle.

One day, as I was unsaddling my horse in the livery stable near my law office, I noted a woebegone stranger wearing an engineer's cap with a celluloid visor and looking as though he hadn't a friend in the world. He asked me timidly if there was any good land up north near my homestead that he could file on.

"No," I said. "There isn't enough level land north of the Yampa River to whip a dog on."

"I was sold out back in Michigan and hoped to find a new home for my large family," he said.

"Family?" I said. "How large is it?"

"Eleven children."

"Are they of school age?" I continued. "Five to twenty-one years old?"

"My oldest daughter is nineteen," he said. "She married a buck Indian but has quit him and lives with us. The youngest is a boy four years old."

Just what we're looking for, I said to myself. Aloud, I said, "We need ten children to have a school district of our own, and we're holding a choice piece of land on Calf Creek for someone to homestead who can furnish the necessary school population. You'll have to see the land before you file, but I'll get you a horse and we'll go there today."

"I can't ride a horse," he said, "because I have a double hernia."

"Then I'll get you a rig and drive you out," I said. "Come over to Shorty's Cafe and I'll buy you a meal."

On the way to Shorty's I noticed that he kept his hand over one pocket. He probably thought I was some kind of confidence man who was going to rob him.

As soon as the meal was served, I went to Shorty's kitchen, where the phone was, and called Jack White. "The Lord has heard our prayer," I told Jack. "I've got a guy here named Jones with eleven head and all but one of school age. Come to town with a rig and we can show him the site."

Jack borrowed Fred Schaefermeyer's old buckboard and a work mare and put a harness on Bosco, a saddle horse that had never been driven before, and came to town. As he was being turned around in the main part of town, Bosco got a rein under his tail and began to put on a rodeo exhibition. There was a fellow in the crowd of onlookers by the name of Ted Barkley, who had the job of "earing down" broncos at the fair for riders to mount. I asked Ted to twist Bosco's ear, and he twisted it so hard that Bosco fell down to his knees in pain.

Jones watched the bucking horse with alarm, but Ted and I half-carried the man to the buckboard and placed him between Jack and myself and set out for Calf Creek. We started for Elkhead at a fast lope—that is, Bosco was in full gallop while the other horse was trotting. Twice we turned over in snowdrifts—tangling horses, harness, and wagon. After we righted the second spill, Jones said, "How much farther is it?"

"Just over three more of those ridges," Jack replied.

"And what does it look like over those ridges?" Jones asked.

"Same as here," Jack answered. "Sagebrush and more oak brush."

"I'm willing to swear I've seen it!" Jones stated firmly. "Please, let's go back."

In the evening I took Mr. Jones to Ezekiel Shelton, the land commissioner, and he filed on the Calf Creek homestead. That made him a resident of Routt County, and I had him sign the petition for the new Elkhead school, listing his ten children of school age. His petition made it mandatory for Mrs. Peck to call an election to form a new school district. All went as planned, and we soon had an election that voted for an Elkhead school district with a school board consisting of myself as president, Jack White as secretary, and Mrs. Charles Fulton as treasurer. This was followed by a second election that made possible the issue of ten thousand dollars worth of school bonds, the proceeds of which could go into a schoolhouse and equipment. Only two problems now faced us: first, to construct a school building that would be the equal of any in Colorado, and second, to get superior unmarried teachers who would inspire the pupils and give our bachelors the "she-stuff" to dream about.

We had decided earlier to close the two little three-month summer schools of our district and create one consolidated school to serve the whole Elkhead district. Every man was in favor of a consolidated school building provided we put it in his own backyard. To settle the matter, an engineer, J. C. Parsons, was employed to make a map showing the place of residence of every child of school age in the district. From that map we found a point that would be approximately an equal distance for all pupils to travel. It was on a hill near a big rimrock stone ledge and belonged to a state school section. Since there was no road to the site, the cowboys got together and built it in one day.

Jones, whose fertility had made it all possible, put up a frame building near the schoolhouse and was promised a job as janitor when the school opened. We succeeded in getting the U.S. Post Office Department to name Elkhead as a post office and let a contract for mail delivery three times a week from Hayden.

Plans were drawn up for a quarried stone building fifty by thirty feet with a full basement and a large one-story room that could be divided into two schoolrooms with a folding partition. Provision was made for a gymnasium in the basement as well as a domestic science room and a large coal-fired furnace. Two stonemasons from Denver, the Frew brothers, were employed to build the walls with rock from the nearby basalt dike; a retired carpenter from Denver was hired by the month to supervise woodwork construction; and I acted as volunteer treasurer and bookkeeper. As there was no place to live near the site, the stonemasons had to camp out. Seeley, the head carpenter, boarded at the Fulton Ranch and walked two miles every day to the site. A well was drilled and water for modern bathroom facilities was brought into the building. The new Elkhead School was modern in every way. It had an electric Delco plant that furnished light, a projector with educational slides donated by the Ford Motor Company, a domestic science room, and a manual training room in the basement.

The building was completed before Christmas of 1915, and the occasion was celebrated by a "housewarming" all-night dance. In order to ensure a big attendance, we arranged a wedding ceremony. Tom McManus, a cowboy who worked for Carpenter and White, was engaged to marry Gertrude Sprague, a young woman who was working for Mrs. William Kleckner on the Bears Ears Ranch. I brought the Hayden minister from town and paid his fee to have the marriage ceremony performed at the Elkhead School during the Christmas dance. To get the day off to a good start, Mrs. Kleckner sent out written invitations for a wedding breakfast to those she considered socially acceptable. It was rumored that she would set the high tone of the event by serving a small glass of wine to each of the guests.

It snowed throughout the previous night. Early the next morning, when I rode over on horseback to help get everything ready, I found that Mrs. Kleckner's team and wagon were having a hard time getting through the snow over the hill to the school. Gertie, the bride-to-be, was pushing the wagon from behind. I put a rope on the end of the wagon tongue and dallied the other end to my saddle horn and let my horse lend power to the climb. It was late in the day by the time the McManuses were united in marriage, and fading daylight threatened the wedding breakfast. But it was considered a great success by all the guests, though some settlers who were not invited wondered what criterion Mrs. Kleckner had used in sending out her invitations.

To supply music for the wedding, we borrowed a phonograph and put on a record of the wedding march before the ceremony. All went well with the breakfast and the wedding, but the snow kept coming. Blankets and food had to be carried into the domestic science room of the school. The entire community came to the dance, scheduled to begin after the ceremony, but the musicians did not arrive. Tom McManus, the groom, produced a harmonica and began playing dance tunes. A chair was put on top of a table at one side of the hall and the crowd kept the groom playing all evening. At midnight I went to the basement to see how preparations were coming along for the midnight lunch. I found the forlorn bride, Gertie, neglected on her wedding night by the popular harmonica player, wrapped up in a red comforter in back of the furnace and sound asleep.

Jack and I got well acquainted with our neighbors, who

stopped by often to lend a hand and see how we were getting along. When the Joneses arrived we all turned out to haul logs for their cabin. Reece Horton loaned them a fresh milk cow. John Adair, who had a huge potato patch, told them that they could have all the potatoes they wanted if they would come and dig them. Wagons and teams were donated to haul their sparse possessions from the Moffat Road in Hayden.

One day the following September, a team and buggy drove up to my cabin. The driver was the beloved physician of Hayden, Doctor Solandt. He responded to calls from settlers within twenty miles of his office and could be counted on for veterinary work when needed. He said that the Jones family on Calf Creek had all come down sick and he was on his way to help. The following day I learned from him that the family had a bad case of amoebic dysentery from eating too much wild meat and improperly cooked vegetables. The youngest boy, four-year-old Herbert, had died and the body was to be buried near the cabin. Since Hayden had no minister at the time, he wanted me to go over to Calf Creek to conduct the funeral service.

Doctor Solandt asked me if I had a Bible. When I said that I had, he told me to go there at once as the child had to be buried that day. He added that I had better get Mrs. Murphy to go with me to help straighten them out on food. He said that Al Galloway was already there making a coffin, and other neighbors would come for the service.

I rode to Dry Fork and found that Mr. Murphy had gone to Rawlins twenty-five miles north to trade a wagonload of oats for his winter's supply of groceries. Mrs. Murphy was alone. When I told her the news, she said, "You catch Old Paint and saddle him, and I'll be ready to go with you." She wrapped up a two-quart jar of rice in a black silk underskirt, which I tied to her saddle. It was a six-mile ride to Calf Creek, and when we got near the Joneses, I could hear Galloway's hammer and saw and the talk of the men who were digging a grave near the creek.

All of the surviving members of the Jones family were huddled inside the cabin, where the little boy's body lay on the bed. Quickly surveying the situation, Mrs. Murphy sent the two older boys to the grave with water for the diggers. Then she took a big kettle of overboiled potatoes from the stove, threw it outdoors, and refilled it with some of the rice from her jar. As this boiled, she ripped the black silk underskirt into strips, had the older girls line the inside of the coffin with it, and fashioned two little pillows to go on each side of the head when the little boy's body was placed inside.

I went off by myself to find in my Bible something appropriate to read. My mother had often told me of a section in the Gospel of John that was called the "consolation chapter," a part of Scripture that was nearly always read at funerals. It began: "Let not your heart be troubled: ye believe in God, believe also in me. In my Father's house are many mansions: if it were not so, I would have told you. I go to prepare a place for you" (John 14:1).

When we were all assembled for the service a great calm prevailed over the listeners seated on logs in front of the cabin. The only hymn that I felt sure enough to lead was "Nearer My God to Thee." For fear of faltering on the words, I wrote them in pencil on the back flyleaf of my Bible. The singing of the hymn was quavering. After the hymn I read the "consolation chapter" and was surprised at what happened when I finished the thirty-first and last verse: "Come let us arise and go hence." At that point the pallbearers jumped up, seized the coffin, and marched off down the hill to the grave. We all followed and I pronounced the passage "Ashes to ashes, and dust to dust." After some wildflowers were strewn on the grave, we departed to our homes.

When the matter of hiring teachers for Elkhead School came up, all of the bachelors felt that they should participate equally with the school board in choosing them. We ran an advertisement in a Denver school magazine for two unmarried teachers at salaries of seventy-five dollars a month, although the usual salary was sixty dollars. The ad read, "No applications will be considered unless accompanied with a recent photograph." The applications—seventeen of them—went to Jack White, who served as secretary for the school board. Jack would call me in Hayden on the phone and say, "Two more applicants today, both blondes." I would reply, "Tack the photos around the wall of your kitchen and let the bachelors vote on them."

Among the applicants were two young eastern women who were 1909 graduates of Smith College in Northampton, Massachusetts. They wrote that they had no experience as teachers and in fact had never done any work for pay. But they had heard about the Western Slope of Colorado and they wanted to get away from the staid pattern of life in New England. Since they did not enclose photos with their applications, we could not consider them. However, I had seen some beautiful Smith girls at Harvard proms and decided to check up on these two. Bob Perry, who ran the family's Oak Creek coal mine, had a sister, Charlotte Perry, who was a 1911 Smith graduate. Bob phoned Charlotte at Steamboat Springs, where she was just starting what became the Perry-Mansfield Dance Camp. Charlotte told Bob that our applicants had been the prettiest and liveliest girls in their class at Smith. That report sounded good to me. Even without photos, I urged the bachelors to take a chance on these two eastern girls because they had better qualifications than the usual run of normal school applicants. So we sent special delivery letters to Rosamond Underwood and Dorothy Woodruff in Auburn, New York, offering them the jobs.

At 11:00 P.M. of an August night in 1916, the two girls arrived from Denver on the Moffat Road. An hour earlier, Hayden's electric lights had gone off and the town was as dark as the inside of a cow. I arranged with the manager of the Hayden Inn to leave a kerosene lamp in the hall with a notice directing them to their room. I also met their train and staggered off carrying their two enormous suitcases. The girls looked a little pale in the vestibule light after their scary ride over Corona Pass. The baggage man had thrown their two big trunks onto the station platform, and the newcomers seemed dubious when I told them that their trunks would be safe sitting unattended through the night. Then I led them to the dark Hayden Inn. The note under the kerosene lamp read: "Try room No. 3. If somebody is sleeping there, try No. 4." The two girls left me and climbed upstairs. I presumed that they found an empty room.

Early next morning, Bob Perry phoned me from the depot. I told him that the girls had arrived.

"What do they look like?" he asked.

I said that I couldn't see them very well in the dark. "They're over at the inn," I said.

"I'll join you there."

I found the girls eating breakfast. Bob was keeping an eye on half a dozen city slickers who were standing around admiring them. I could see by the glazed look on Bob's face as he stared at Rosamond that he was already smitten. He took me aside.

TOP: *Elkhead schoolhouse upon completion, fall 1915. In front, from left to right, are Ros Perry, Belle Carpenter, and Paroda Fulton.* LEFT: *Farrington's sister, Ruth, brands a calf as Ferry holds it down.*

TOP: *Annie Elmer at the Salinas (Calif.) rodeo, about 1916.* BOTTOM: *Robert M. ("Bob") Perry (left), his wife Marjorie, and Rosamond Underwood Perry at the Moffat Mine in Oak Creek, about 1917.*

"Watch her mail," he said. "Let me know if some man is writing to her."

I got one of the livery stable boys to drive the girls in a buckboard from Hayden to the Harrison Ranch on Calf Creek, where they were to board three and a half miles from Elkhead School. I picked up their first mail as they scrambled into the buckboard. A bunch of letters postmarked Michigan were addressed to Dorothy in masculine handwriting. Rosamond had only one letter in a woman's hand—probably from her mother, as I later told Bob Perry.

When I gave the girls their mail I invited them to my thirtieth birthday party on August 10—a sort of "coming out" party to present them to the Elkhead community. My cabin was five miles from the Harrison Ranch, and I told them to borrow saddle horses from the Harrisons. The girls said that they would not be able to come to my party because they could not dance in the heavy canvas-divided skirts that they wore on horseback. I told them to put their dance clothes in a flour sack, tie the sack to the saddle, and change clothes at the party.

"Where do we change?" Rosamond asked anxiously.

"My cabin will be full of people dancing," I said, "but there's plenty of oak brush outside and you can find a place."

They must have decided to take a chance on the uncouth ways of the wild and woolly West because they indeed came to the party. As it happened, I was celebrating my birthday by building a bathroom with a flush toilet, using water piped down from the spring. Modern plumbing was a novelty at Elkhead. Everywhere guests rushed up to me and said: "Happy Birthday! Show me the flush toilet!" I wondered if our eastern ladies had ever heard such a birthday greeting in Auburn.

Bob Perry arrived at the party from his home near the coal mine he owned at Oak Creek. It was plain that his only interest was Rosamond Underwood. However, Bob had never learned square dancing, and the cowboys kept the new teachers busy on the floor all night. At sunup, Rosamond and Dorothy got on their horses for the ride back to the Harrison Ranch. Rosamond said, "That's the first time I ever saw the sun set one day and rise for another with no sleep in between."

During the weeks before the new school began in September, our teachers seemed to adjust very well to the perils of western living. Rosamond recalled later that she arrived at Elkhead walking on air. Bob Perry had proposed to her. She had fallen in love with him and had accepted his proposal. Then, as she walked to the school on a golden Monday, she found a sheriff's notice tacked on the front door. It announced a reward of $1,000 for information leading to the arrest of the Oak Creek men who had kidnapped Bob Perry and were holding him for $25,000 ransom in gold coin.

I learned of the kidnapping when Bob's father, Sam Perry, phoned me at Hayden from the home of Gerald J. Hughes, Jr., a prominent Denver lawyer. While Mr. Perry was dining with Hughes in Denver, a special delivery ransom letter arrived, directing Bob's father to deliver the $25,000 in gold personally within three days to a spot called Coal Gulch near Oak Creek. He was to ride there alone on his own white horse. Gerald Hughes, a director of Denver's First National Bank, hurriedly got the gold and ordered a Moffat Road train loaded with the ransom and armed with five detectives from the Denver police force to head full steam for Oak Creek.

Mr. Perry sent the same express to pick me up at Hayden after it reached Oak Creek. Meanwhile, I had organized a cowboy posse. We followed several false leads which put us on the third day at Doctor Cole's home in Yampa, nine miles south of Oak Creek. That was the deadline set by Bob's kidnappers, who threatened to murder him if they had not received the ransom. At lunch, as the members of the posse ate glumly, the phone rang. Mr. Perry jumped to answer it and shrieked, "It's Bob!" Tears rolled down his cheeks as he said that Bob had escaped from his kidnappers and had run to the phone at the Ben Male coal mine near Oak Creek.

We piled into Mr. Perry's car and found Bob hale and hearty though sporting three days of whiskers. He told us that two Greek miners had tied a gunnysack over his head and led him with a rope to Coal Gulch. They took turns sleeping as they guarded him. After the second day, he noticed that one of the guards kept nodding off, with his head resting on the hand that held his rifle. For hours, even with his hands tied behind his back, Bob considered ways to attack the dozing kidnapper. Then, on the day of the deadline, he decided it was now or never. He backed up to the nodding guard, grabbed his rifle with both hands, felt the binds break, and shouted, "Run or I'll kill you!" The man woke up and took off. The second kidnapper lunged at

Bob with a long knife, but his victim whirled with the rifle and pulled the trigger. The man fell, wounded in the neck. Bob remembered throwing away the rifle and galloping out of Coal Gulch, clearing the tops of the thick brush cover as easily as a deer. He did not stop running until he reached a telephone.

The next day the Routt County coroner went to Coal Gulch and found the dead body of the kidnapper who had gone at Bob with the long knife. Three days later the second kidnapper was arrested and jailed in Steamboat Springs. I went there with Bob to identify him, and the Greek greeted Bob with a smile. In turn, Bob shook hands with him and called him Jim. At his trial, the jury found Jim guilty of kidnapping and armed robbery. He was sentenced to the Canon City penitentiary for "life and seven years."

Recovering from the shock of the kidnapping, Rosamond announced her engagement to Bob and said that they would live in Oak Creek after their marriage. Dorothy Woodruff was to marry Lemuel S. Hillman, a young Michigan banker. So the Elkhead bachelors knew that they were losing both of their schoolmarms.

The two Smith College girls turned out to be fine teachers during their year at Elkhead School. The winter of 1916–17 was a time of heavy snow. On their twice daily trip of over three miles to school, the girls hung snowshoes on the necks of their horses to be used when the snow was too deep for the horses. Yet they missed only one day of school. They started a Girl Scout troop and put on plays for the entertainment of the community. They persuaded a homesteader from Russia to teach a class in cobbling. When the school year ended, just before I began military service in the spring of 1917, the Elkhead School Board gave each of the girls gold medals with a replica of the school on one side. On the reverse side were inscribed the words "For bravery in attendance and loyalty in work."

SEVEN

Lieutenant Carpenter
and World War I

None of us around Hayden dreamed that the clouds of war gathering over Europe could ever cross our Big Divide to disturb the back country peace of Routt County. But we began taking the Kaiser seriously on May 7, 1915, when a German submarine sank the British steamer *Lusitania* with the loss of 1,198 lives. I read in our weekly *Routt County Republican* Woodrow Wilson's neutrality statements and applauded his reelection as president in 1916 with the slogan, He kept us out of war. But I wondered how my Princeton mentor was standing the awful pressure of his job after April 6, 1917, when Congress declared war on Germany.

When America declared war against Germany and Italy, a wave of patriotism swept the nation. Volunteer enlistment swamped the army recruiting offices. Caught in the fever, I spent six weeks in a "citizens military training camp" at Fort Douglas near Salt Lake City which was set up to prepare men to become commissioned officers if the need arose for a large army. Soon after this training, President Wilson and Newton D. Baker, secretary of war, advocated a selective service law, empowering the government to select men from eighteen to forty-five years old for military service and to defer from service citizens needed to support the war effort in other ways.

As war-torn Europe became more and more dependent on food shipments from the United States and Canada, the statement "Food will win the war" was commonly heard. Though

Routt County was hay country, the soaring price of wheat inspired Hayden farmers to study dry farming, a new method of tillage—as practiced on the plains of eastern Colorado—that included crop rotation and furrowing to conserve snow water. Local farmers hoped that the new method might make crop farming possible in the region's short seventy-five day growing season and scant rainfall of seventeen inches annually.

The Selective Service procedure for deferment from military service for men in occupations deemed essential to the war effort did not recognize agricultural workers as vital enough to be deferred. To remedy that omission, I organized the Routt County Farmers' Council and presented its plan of operation in Denver to Governor Julius C. Gunter. The governor gave us a committee and an office in the State Capitol building, but it soon became apparent that the committee would do little except write verbose letters to the editor, few of which were ever printed. So, relying on my father's oft-told advice ("When you want something done *now*, do it yourself and don't rely on others"), I took the train and went to Washington.

When I got there, I enlisted the help of Colorado's congressman-at-large, Edward J. Keating. I saw also a lawyer from Glenwood Springs, Congressman Edward T. Taylor, who was serving his fourth term in the House of Representatives. Though he was a Democrat and I was a Republican, we were good friends.

Ordinarily, congressmen and senators had access to any governmental department. Now, in wartime, the city had become an armed citadel. When Congressman Keating and I went to the War Department, a soldier with a bayonet on his rifle stopped us at the gate and refused us entrance. After several higher-ups refused to see us, Congressman Keating turned to me and said, "There's no chance of seeing anybody who could change the draft regulations unless we get up to God. Ferry, didn't you tell me that you used to know the president?"

When I explained my work on club reform with Woodrow Wilson at Princeton, Keating led me to the White House to see Joe Tumulty, the president's private secretary. Tumulty took my name and address and said he would let me know if I could see the president. The next day a notice arrived requesting my presence at the White House at 10:00 A.M. Ushered into the Oval Office, I saw President Wilson all dressed up in a white linen suit but looking much older than he had at Princeton in 1910.

"What brings you to Washington, Farrington?" he said with a smile. As I explained my mission, he quickly grasped it. "What you want done," he said, "will have to be agreed upon by three departments—Agriculture, Labor, and War." Then, picking up a note pad which bore an engraving of the White House on its sheets, he wrote, signed, and dated the following note: "Please consider the bearer, Farrington R. Carpenter's recommendation for amending the deferments from military service."

I took little time in showing the president's note to the soldier at the front gate of the War Department. In a few minutes, I found myself in the waiting room of Newton D. Baker, the secretary of war. He was in conference with a delegation of French generals who had just arrived in the country to persuade the government that the U. S. regular army should be sent to France to fill the great gaps in the Allied defense army.

After I had waited half an hour, a tall, handsome young man with curly black hair called my name and took me aside. He was about my age, and something about his dress and stride made me think of the typical Cambridge undergraduate. I asked him where he had gone to college.

"Harvard, 1910," he said. "My name's Walter Lippmann. I'm a journalist working here as Secretary Baker's assistant. The secretary is tied up with the French officers. Would you tell me what you want to see him about?" I explained to Lippmann my deferment idea for farm workers, and he promised to pass it on to Secretary Baker.

I then called on David F. Houston, the secretary of agriculture, who spent most of the meeting giving me copies of his speeches. I felt that I was wasting both my time and Houston's. My next call, however, was in the office of William B. Wilson, the secretary of labor, who passed me along to one of the most impressive men I have ever met. His name was Samuel Gompers, and though he was approaching seventy, I was struck by the surging vitality of this stocky, London-born cigarmaker who had created that giant instrument of trade unionism in the United States, the American Federation of Labor.

President Wilson's so-called Labor Czar greeted me warmly and, like the president, easily understood the reason for my mission. As we were talking, an official came in and said, "The committee is waiting for you on the sixth floor." Gompers got up, put his arm around my shoulders, and said, "Mr. Carpenter, I want you to come with me to this committee meeting. It has to do with your concern."

About twenty people were seated around a large, oval table in the committee room. Only one vacant seat remained, and it was next to the only woman in the room. I took the vacant seat and introduced myself. The woman was handsome, in her late thirties, and had the outdoor look of a rancher. I recognized her at once as Jeannette Rankin, the famous suffragette and member of congress from Montana, the first woman ever elected to Congress, and the only member of Congress to vote against our entry into the war.

As chairman of the meeting, Samuel Gompers opened the proceedings by introducing President Wilson's food administrator, the solemn, reserved Herbert Hoover, who described his plan for stimulating food production and for promoting voluntary meatless and wheatless days. In his remarks, Hoover mentioned ways to increase crop acreage but felt that they were too slow to meet the emergency. "I think I know the American farmer," he said in conclusion. "A higher price is what will immediately increase the production of the prime product—wheat. The price of wheat is now eighty cents a bushel. Next year it will be $1.75 per bushel. At that price the American farmer will meet the crisis soon enough to meet the need."

Despite having seen and talked with everyone in Washington who was in position to bring about deferments for food producers, I returned home with no firm commitment for changes in the draft regulations. Back in Denver I found that the state authorities were unwilling to adopt the Routt County Farmers' Council plan. As secretary of the council, I kept in touch, through Edward Keating, with the secretary of agriculture, and I spent weeks on the phone lining up local people. The most difficult to crack were the legalists in Denver who could not act without a law to do it by. I was surprised at how easily big businessmen in Denver were chilled by an ominous look on some lawyer's face over questions of legality.

While I was busy with the farmers' council, patriotic fever had developed all over Routt County. A mass meeting had been held and a majority had voted to raise a company of cavalry volunteers and attach it to the Colorado National Guard, which was then being put into national service. As one who had had military training at Fort Douglas, I was elected captain of the company. I declined the honor, explaining that cavalry was not being used in this war and that everyone should wait for his number to be called by the draft board for military service. As I was unmarried and of military age, I found myself in the embarrassing position of being regarded as a draft dodger. I went to the county sheriff, Emery Clark, and asked that I be selected to go in the first call for Routt County draftees.

The call came on October 2, 1917, and I went to Steamboat Springs to join twenty-eight other first draftees in a parade down the main street heading for the morning train to Denver. At the Steamboat station a band was playing "Over There" and one old man I knew had tears rolling down his cheeks. He was Colonel James H. Crawford, a Civil War veteran who had founded Steamboat Springs in 1875.

Our destination on that troop trip was for training at Camp Funston, Kansas. We had a baggage car for a kitchen in the center of the train. The traveling ration was hardtack (just like thick educator biscuits—and good), bread, jam, coffee, corned-beef hash, and canned tomatoes. At Funston no uniforms were available so each draftee was given a brown coverall. There were no rifles to drill with. Two privates who were carpenters sawed out rifles from lumber and these were used for drill purposes. Although it was disappointing to be without uniforms and to have to go around in ill-fitting coveralls, the good humor of the men kept our morale up. For example, at one 6:00 A.M. line-up in front of the barracks, a cold Kansas wind was blowing. The officer in charge noticed that one of our shortest soldiers, standing at the end of the line, was shivering.

"What's the matter with you?" the officer asked him.

"Oh, Lieutenant," he said, "I got caught in the draft."

At another morning line-up, all draftees with previous military experience were asked to move three steps forward. The commanding officer then went to each of them and inquired about their previous military experience. One man had been to Culver Military School in Indiana, and he was therefore appointed first sergeant. When I told the commanding officer of my training at Fort Douglas, he made me supply sergeant.

After several months of training at Camp Funston, five of our company were chosen to go to the Third Officers' Training Corps at Camp Gordon, Georgia. I was one of them. The war was on in earnest now. When the troop train taking me to Georgia got to Slater, Missouri, the whole town was at the depot cheering and serenading us and handing out homemade pies and papers and magazines. I never saw such a welcome—with pretty girls running up for kisses and asking if we knew so and so back in Colorado. The mayor of Slater passed out cigarettes and cigars, and one old duck exhorted us to get the Kaiser's private parts and bring it back to Slater to pickle.

I noticed on that troop trip that the home folks were far more stirred up about the war in France than the draftees. We hardly ever talked about it or discussed who was right or wrong. As for the Missouri train itself, the journey was pretty rocky but in no way as bumpy as the ride on that frightening Moffat Road from Denver rolling over Corona Pass at twelve thousand feet above sea level. The Missouri country was beautiful and we eventually went on into Indiana and Tennessee. Everyone stopped whatever they were doing to wave at us—kids at crossings and old people on their back porches waving flags. It was enough to bring tears to our eyes.

I spent about two months in officers' training at Camp Gordon. The discipline and work routine of my unit were by far the strictest I had ever known. When I graduated in June 1918, we were commissioned second lieutenants and assigned to camps all over the country to train the big army that would go to Europe to bolster the battered Allied forces. I was assigned a squad of eight men whom I drilled, ate meals with, and shared life with in the barracks. They were from four different European countries, and I had to censor their mail. I was amazed at the loyalty to the United States expressed in the letters that these foreigners wrote to their families.

When I received my commission I was ordered to report to the commanding officer of the student training unit at the University of Arkansas at Fayetteville. My detachment of three hundred men was clothed, fed, and trained to become Radio Signal Corps operators. They spent half a day in classrooms and half a day in military training. The man in charge was Captain Block, a graduate of the Second Officers Training Corps.

Captain Block was an extraordinary officer. Arriving at Fayetteville, I had put on the brass bars showing that I was a second lieutenant. I was proud of my new status and anxious to see how I would be recognized as a commissioned officer—not just another draftee. On my way across campus to the headquarters office, I passed several privates but none of them saluted me. When I knocked on Captain Block's office door, I heard a loud "Come on in!" A large man, Captain Block was seated in a chair with his blouse unbuttoned. Since I had been reading up on military courtesy, I stood at attention and with a salute said, "Sir, Lieutenant Carpenter reporting for duty."

"Sit down," he said. "We don't bother about saluting here."

Block had been the boss of an oil drilling crew in Oklahoma and boasted that he could handle all kinds of men—Indians, Chinese, Mexicans, and Americans. He appointed me as his administrative assistant, and when I told him that an officer sent by the inspector general of the army would be around to see us some day, he replied, "I'll take care of him when he gets here."

I had the duty of leading early morning calisthenics and close-order drills. The detachment was quartered in a college dormitory, and the soldiers brought all kinds of musical instruments, furniture, and barbershop posters to their rooms—violating all the army's rules for behavior in the barracks. One day a telegram came from a commanding officer in another detachment in Missouri stating that the inspector would be with us the next day. I knew our quarters would put him into a rage, so I asked Captain Block's advice.

"Take everything but the prescribed beds, footlockers, and chairs," he said, "and pile them where the inspector can't see them."

The men willingly cooperated when I explained the captain's scheme. All went well with the inspection until the inspector came to the locked room in which the men had piled their junk.

"What's in there?" he demanded.

"It belongs to the university," I replied.

"Don't tell me the university has rooms the army can't inspect!" the man roared.

I said I would get the key and ran to tell Block the situation. Without a moment's hesitation, the captain said, "Have the bugler sound the fire call." A fire call, of course, required everyone to pick up his rifle and fall into line in front of the building. The

LEFT: *Second Lieutenant (Infantry) Farrington R. Carpenter, June 1918.* BOTTOM: *On leave after graduation from officer training in 1918, Farrington stands with members of the Wilkins family at the Dawson Ranch. From left to right are Ralph, Laura (daughter of John Dawson), Farrington, and Earl. The children are Edwina (tallest), Charles, and Foreman White.*

RIGHT: *Eunice Pleasant at Elkhead School, 1920, before her marriage to Farrington Carpenter.* BOTTOM: *Maybell store, 1919. John Joe Pleasant is the child on the left.*

men acted with astonishing speed and the inspector was so pleased with the performance that he forgot all about the locked room.

One of my duties was to read the articles of war to the recruits. The penalties for infractions of these articles were nearly always "death or as a court-martial shall direct." When I was halfway through this lecture one day, Captain Block appeared. He jumped up on the rostrum and said to the assembled recruits: "These articles of war are for someone else. I'm the court here, and if anyone wants to dispute my authority, just take your jacket off and step up here and we'll see who's the best man." No one doubted that he was a natural leader, and more than one soldier hoped that he would have a leader like Captain Block in combat.

On the Fourth of July the detachment was asked to march in the town parade, but when the captain found out that his company was to follow the city's fire department, he changed all the plans and took our detachment to the head of the line. "Nobody can march ahead of the army," he said.

One day the first families of Fayetteville gave a reception at the country club for the commissioned personnel, who consisted of the captain, his wife, and three of us lieutenants. Captain Block got angered at something his young wife said or did and threatened her with a spanking. Needless to say, the town's society people were shocked by his ungenteel behavior. Yet once, after a committee of ladies had called on Captain Block, I found him blushing scarlet. When I asked him what they had discussed, he said, "The committee wanted me to tell them how to prevent war babies."

Though many draftees yearn to experience combat abroad, they find that such assignments are made by higher authorities. If I had not been sent to officers' training camp I would have seen combat in France with the Eighty-ninth Division of the Army. The Eighty-ninth had a distinguished career on the battlefield, and I would have been proud to have been one of them. But if I had any special military qualifications they involved training recruits, and that was what my superiors decided that I should do.

After four months at Fayetteville, I was ordered in September 1918 to report to the president of Howard Payne College in Brownwood, Texas, as commanding officer of the Student Army

Training Corps (SATC). Southwest of Dallas, Brownwood turned out to be a pleasant town of thirteen thousand people in a rich agricultural area which included a number of oil wells and a few other industries. The place was spiked with church steeples rising above the pecan and walnut trees.

I discovered that Howard Payne College was a coeducational Baptist institution with 1,200 students. It was set in a handsome tree-shaded campus spotted with statues of deer, antelope, and moose. The SATC had been set up by the government in some four hundred colleges to train men eighteen years of age and over who were high school graduates. The training would not only prepare the students for college but also qualify them for military service as officers. As a second lieutenant, I was a commanding officer with three other lieutenants as junior officers. I had just turned thirty-two and felt that I was taking on a big responsibility.

The SATC was officially organized on October 1, 1918, with 136 recruits inducted on that day by local draft boards. The recruits, many of them Texans, arrived ready to go, but no equipment or uniforms awaited them. The regular college had been shut down temporarily, and I asked the college president, Dr. Tolman, if I could borrow a typewriter until my office supplies came. He sent me one and with it a typist—the dean of Howard Payne College! Everybody stood around waiting for my orders as though I were in charge of Brownwood and about to declare martial law.

My first chore was to make a stump speech to the citizens explaining what we were doing there. I told them we would be training officers and technical specialists. I added that their community had turned over part of Howard Payne College to show their support of the government in creating an army to end the war. I also met with a committee of the Chamber of Commerce to discuss the new barracks on campus for the trainees. The organization had collected $7,500 from the tight-fisted old Brownwood merchants, and they were busy figuring out how to get most of it back. It reminded me of the town council meetings in Hayden. Later I met the college trustees, who were as solemn as Mormon elders. When they learned that as quartermaster and commanding officer I had $5,000 on deposit for expenses, the two banker trustees rolled their eyes. One of them invited me over to sit on his front porch and gave me a glass of lemonade and a sack of Ben Davis apples. He told me to come around to his bank the next day and he would fix me up nicely.

As soon as I could get my men in uniform, I led a parade down Fiske Street through town. For the parade I got the Boy Scouts, the high school cadet corps, and the Brownwood Fire Department. After exercises in front of the half-built barracks, my men hoisted the flag. Having just learned how to play "To the Colors," the buglers had some trouble hitting the high notes. After a short drill, the men filed off to mess, which had been set up in the basement of the girls' dormitory.

As commanding officer I had no place to live, but Dr. Tolman made room for me with his family on the ground floor of the dormitory. I did not wait for an order to move in, for as a representative of the United States government, I felt I was in charge. I appointed a local physician as surgeon for the corps, leased a thousand-acre tract as a target field, and contacted the local Red Cross unit for nurses as needed. I imagined myself to be the skinny dictator of a great region, with Uncle Sam paying the bills for my smallest whim. I assigned duties to my three assistant second lieutenants, named noncommissioned officers, and set up my office with a head clerk, stenographers, and a bonded treasurer.

It is well that I got things organized in a hurry. In a few days I had to quarantine the whole corps because of the virulent influenza epidemic that swept over the nation. By October 10, 1918, I had 122 cases in my corps, and 99 men in bed too sick to care for themselves. Our barracks was turned into a hospital with nurses from the Red Cross.

The flu epidemic was bad enough, but the mothers who poured in to comfort their sick boys were worse than the disease. We could not allow the mothers into the quarantined, homemade hospital. Even the nurses and doctors had to have entrance orders signed by me. One mother got by the guard and pulled a bottle of grape juice out of her bodice, uncorked it, and let all those sick boys drink out of the same bottle.

My most acute visitor problem involved a Baptist preacher who was a college trustee and thought he owned the place. He wanted to cure the ailing trainees by praying over them. He criticized everything I was doing and let me know that he believed I was hauling out the bodies of dead boys every night to the city dump. Except for the preacher, most of the parents cooperated with me and trusted me to notify them if one of their boys was in danger. Though two of the boys died of the flu, I was satisfied that the doctors and nurses had done everything possible to save them.

I never contracted the flu myself, even though I made it a custom to tour the hospital each day and speak to every patient. It helped their morale. And though they never knew it, the men bolstered my own morale as well. For one thing, they never lost their sense of humor. This was clear when the local newspaper ran an ad calling for bids for the service of a mortician. Of the three morticians in Brownwood, only one had a hearse with rubber tires. After the ad appeared, as I walked through the wards, the patients greeted me with big smiles and said, "Oh, Lieutenant, for gosh sakes, get me the firm with the rubber-tired hearse!"

By October 14 the worst of the epidemic was over and I could resume lectures and drill with 173 men on the roster. I felt that the strict quarantine and dieting had brought the results that we had hoped for. I was also pleased to receive my promotion to first lieutenant. At the same time, my work load was eased when the army sent me another secretary and a first lieutenant as singing master to improve the spirits of the corps.

The song leader, a former teacher at Choate Prep School in Connecticut, had a marvelous aptitude for his work. When I presented him to the corps, all the men looked glum and disinterested. He started off with "Little Liza Jane," which had an easy lilt, and followed it with the fast-moving "K-K-K-Katy." All of a sudden the men were with him, blasting out "Over There," "Pack Up Your Troubles in Your Old Kit Bag," and "Mr. Zip, Zip, Zip, with Your Hair Cut Just as Short as Mine." From then on, the corps called their song leader Mr. Zip.

The man was a born comic. One day he announced a "poetry class." Most of the corps attended, suspecting a joke. Mr. Zip, dressed in a preacher's black robe, intoned his "poem" in grave Bible Belt tones:

> Our Father who art in Washington,
> Hallowed be Thy Name,
> We Drove the Hun
> Into Kingdom Come;
> Thy work was done on Earth
> As it should be in heaven.

Give us this day
All our back pay,
And lead us not into the
Army of Occupation,
But deliver us from all
Details and Fatigues.

And forgive us all our AWOLs,
As we forgive them with bars,
Who have them charged against us;
For Thou hast the power to
Return us to our homes,
And leave us there forever.

Amen

Thereafter the days passed quickly with drills and a few field trips. On November 11, 1918, the armistice was signed and World War I was over. We celebrated the event with a parade and the presentation of a flag to the corps by the Daughters of the American Revolution.

The men then approached me asking to wind up their tour of duty with a dance. Howard Payne College had a longstanding tradition against dancing, and Dr. Tolman told me that if he allowed a dance it would break the tradition. He forbade the college coeds to attend, but the soldiers went ahead and invited all the waitresses from the Harvey Eating House near the railroad station. As it turned out, however, many coeds attended the dance by sneaking down the fire escapes of the girls' dormitory. My own date was the daughter of a leading merchant who drove me to the dance in a snappy blue Chandler. Her social standing in Brownwood was one of the best, and her presence gave prestige to the whole affair.

I spent until December 7, 1918, completing records for the mustering out of the corps. On that date all the men were discharged except myself. I had to wait until January before all the records could be checked and I could hurry to Denver, where I soon caught the first train for Hayden.

When I returned to Hayden in 1919, the Elkhead School Board asked me to find a new teacher for the school. At a dance in Hayden I met Eunice Pleasant, who was three years my junior. She had come from Kansas to visit her brother Floyd, a banker in Craig, and had taught school in seven different Kansas towns. At first she refused to stay in Colorado since she was under contract to teach in Kansas. However, she did agree to ask for a release, and it was granted. The winning card for getting her consent to teach at Elkhead was a new, fully equipped teacher's house that went along with the salary. Tired of living in boardinghouses with other teachers, she wanted a home of her own. At her request, two high school pupils lived in the house on weekdays and returned home for the weekends.

Of all the single young women I had known in Routt and Moffat counties, Eunice was in a class by herself. As our daughter described her many years later, she was "a handsome woman of top-drawer, gold-plated academic and intellectual attainments." Born in a family of seven children in the small town of Lyndon, Kansas, where her father was a lawyer, Eunice taught school to earn her way through Kansas University, majoring in English and graduating Phi Beta Kappa.

Fresh out of the army, I taught soldiering and calisthenics at Elkhead while Eunice handled the high school subjects. Working together as we did, of course, the inevitable happened, and by Easter 1920 we were engaged. On August 28, 1920, we were married in Floyd Pleasant's home in Craig and set up housekeeping in my homestead cabin at Oak Point. While I commuted every day to my law office in Hayden, Eunice quickly turned cowgirl and rode the pastures and range for Carpenter and White. She saw to it that the gates were shut, that the bulls were scattered, and that no outside bulls were among our cows. In addition, she filled the salt boxes and kept the water holes open.

H. B. ("Johnny") Pleasant, Eunice's brother, had opened a store in Maybell, a small desert town west of Craig that had been named for the two granddaughters of Maybell's first postmaster, John Banks. In June 1921 Johnny came to Hayden to tell me that the Yampa River had flooded out the Maybell irrigation ditch. He wanted to know if the town could issue bonds to restore the ditches. I phoned Dr. Charles Lory, head of the State Agricultural College at Fort Collins, who said that if we called it a "scholastic project" he could send Aggie students and faculty to make plans for the ditch.

When the Denver bankers refused to issue bonds for the ditch, I went to an acquaintance of mine, Mrs. Verner Z. Reed, the widow of the Cripple Creek multimillionaire and Wyoming oilman. Known in Denver as "Lady Bountiful," she had just given Denver $50,000 for a library. Mrs. Reed agreed to take the entire $30,000 bond issue, and with her sponsorship the Maybell ditch was built and the bonds were paid off at maturity. When Johnny Pleasant burned the bonds, no community in Colorado was prouder than little Maybell out there on the edge of the Moffat County desert.

EIGHT

Doctor Solandt's Hospital

There comes a time when every young man loses interest in the pleasant preoccupations of adolescence and yearns to come to grips with the achievement of his adult dreams and ambitions. I began this process after I returned from nineteen months of military service and married Eunice Pleasant. I knew that my father would be retiring soon from the management of his successful shoe factory in Holland, Michigan, and that he was hoping I might take his place. I loved my father and owed him a great deal, but I had known ever since my days as a teen-aged cowboy in New Mexico that the urban life was not for me. Yet I was also aware that the joys of rural life had severe limitations. Most of the amenities that city dwellers took for granted—hot and cold running water, plumbing, electricity, paved roads, and central heating—were lacking in Routt County, and even in 1920 telephones in the region were rare. An occasional all-night square dance served as our entertainment, and our most exciting event was the biweekly arrival of the Moffat train from Denver.

As I watched our young people leave Hayden for the higher wages and modern comforts of the cities, I realized that something had to be done to make our little town of four hundred people in the Yampa River valley a more attractive place in which to live and prosper. I had no idea what our first need was or how to satisfy it. Then one day something happened that solved my problem of priorities. In the early summer of 1921, Eunice announced that she was pregnant, and the joy I felt at her announcement was followed by shock. My mother, I recalled, had been able to give birth comfortably and safely in Evanston, with doctors stopping at our house daily, squads of nurses on hand during the delivery, and a room reserved for her mother at the neighborhood hospital in case of an emergency. In contrast, there was no building in Routt or Moffat counties—an area as large as the entire state of New Jersey—that could be classified as a hospital. Oak Point was ten miles by primitive dirt road from Hayden, and in the dead of winter, when our first-born was now expected, we were usually snowed in. Even without snow, the ride to Hayden in a jolting buggy might bring an early and inopportune arrival of the baby. Of course, I thought: Hayden's first urgent need was a modern hospital.

Our beloved community doctor, J. V. Solandt, was a man of ideals as well as service. He had arrived from Canada to settle in Hayden in 1898. Thereafter, day and night, winter and summer, his buggy, his cutter (with a high back to keep the snow off his neck), his saddle horse, and his skis helped him cover this vast territory to relieve the sick and suffering. The tales of his trips and his heroism were augmented by stories of his kindly ways. His career ended when, on his way home from Steamboat Springs, where he had taken a patient, the lights on his Model T Ford went out on Trull Hill. His car ran off the road, turned over, and pinned the doctor underneath. He died in a few hours. For three years following Doctor Solandt's death, the people of the town and countryside were doctorless except as they availed themselves of a physician in Mount Harris, a mining town seven miles away, or relied on the astonishingly efficacious prescriptions and advice of the Hayden druggist.

With no doctor on hand, I prepared for our baby's arrival as best as I could. I bought everything on the shelves of the Hayden drugstore that our druggist said applied to birth and babies, and I read all the available how-to-do-it books on the subject. Lucius Hallett, a good friend who was on the board of St. Luke's hospital in Denver, sent along a nurse from its obstetrical ward to be with us in a house we had rented in Hayden.

The great event occurred on January 27, 1922—a day on which a big snowstorm had blockaded the highway. Dr. D. L. Whittiker, the coal company physician at Mount Harris, had come to Hayden by a little hand-propelled flatcar on the railroad tracks. Since both Eunice and I were in our early thirties and as this was our first child, we were apprehensive about complications. It was an all-night ordeal, and many times I doubted if any baby could have survived the pulling to which ours was subjected. When the cry of our infant boy was finally heard, I was ready to sign an oath of celibacy.

Eunice and I named our son Edward F. Carpenter after his grandfather. When I had recovered a bit from the experience, and Eunice and I returned with the baby to Oak Point, I planned to hire a cowboy to ride the pastures and leave Eunice free to look after Edward and do the housework. But she loved being a cowhand, so we hired a housekeeper to care for the baby and Eunice continued handling the cattle, which she did better than any cowboy I ever knew.

Meanwhile I lost no time in discussing our hospital needs with my Hayden friends. Within a week the Ladies Aid Society of the Congregational Church offered to serve a dinner at which a hospital proposition could be publicly acted upon. During the dinner the name of Dr. J. V. Solandt was suggested as a suitable one for the proposed building. The idea of making our hospital a memorial to this beloved man appealed to the old-timers, who had benefited from his long years of service.

Acting as moderator for the dinner meeting, I was well schooled in the technique of raising funds for charity, having seen it done often in my home church back in Evanston. There we had had a deacon named Dorr Kimball, who always presided on such occasions. He had called his method "the big blackboard way." It consisted of facing the audience with a blackboard upon which pledges were recorded. The deacon always entered his own name as the first contributor; then, to get an immediate response from the audience, he followed it with several other pledges he had received in advance. In that way he created a feeling that there was a goal to be reached and that it was up to everyone to achieve it.

I decided to follow the deacon's example of group psychology, and it worked like magic. Jack White and I each led off with $1,000 pledges which were followed by others that we had obtained prior to the meeting. In less than two hours, $17,500 had been pledged by over four hundred subscribers with subscriptions ranging from $10 to $1,500. Committees were appointed to call on absent citizens for more pledges.

A not-for-profit corporation was formed to manage the project. It had a board of twelve directors elected by the donors, and each donor was allowed as many votes as the dollars that he or she had contributed. In this way, the donors who gave the most decided who should govern the project. At the first meeting of the directors, I was elected chairman and given the job of business manager to get it into operation.

In order to transform the undertaking into a reality, Jack White and I took a bundle of stakes and a hatchet to the top of a mesa that overlooked the town from its south side. Here we marked out a two-block area of town lots donated to the hospital project by an owner who was tired of paying taxes on them. We then staked out a building site fifty feet long and thirty feet wide on the edge of a hill facing the town, and Lloyd Smith brought his teams, a plow, and some scrapers to excavate the cellar. We figured that the dirt removed for the building would provide a roadway, but unfortunately it all rolled to the bottom of the hill and left the building site with no room for an entrance. The only way to enter the building was through a back door, where the entrance remains to this day.

With the site staked out, every artisan and contractor in town wanted to participate in the project. Plasterers, carpenters, and electricians came forward who would work on the building and take half their pay in cash and half in hospital stock. Merchants procured hardware and material at cost, and Gus Rosenberg, who owned a concrete mixer, agreed to mix all the concrete if the hospital furnished the cement. In addition, John Parker, who had a brick kiln in west Hayden, furnished filler bricks at cost; schoolchildren subscribed for face bricks, which had to be imported at five cents each; Fred Vest and his son, who were contractors, offered to work in their slack time if the hospital gave them meal tickets at a Hayden restaurant; and George and Harry Watson, ranchers who were graduates of the Massachusetts Institute of Technology, wired the building for free. It all resembled an old-fashioned barn raising.

Lucius Hallett, my Denver hospital expert, had advised us to get an oversized furnace and hot water boiler. He warned that the lack of heat and hot water led to proverbial complaints by nurses and patients. Thus, we purchased an extra-large furnace and hot water boiler from the Boulder Plumbing and Supply House at a cost of $14,000. When that bill could not be paid and the company's attorney, Mr. Hutchinson, threatened to sue the hospital, I went to Boulder to pacify the owners. I told them that as the only lawyer in the community I prepared nearly every resident's last will and testament. I agreed to put a sign in my office stating that anyone leaving a legacy of $1,000 or more to the hospital would be charged no fee for a will. All legacies would be put into a special account, and the money from this account would go only toward the payment of outstanding hospital facility bills. Those who accepted my offer inserted a provision that I remain as secretary and treasurer of the hospital until its debts were paid in full.

The compromise worked out well and much sooner than I had expected. An elderly ranchman by the name of Luke Roland, who had a small spread on William's Fork, came to my office one day and asked me to prepare his will. He was divorced and his wife had moved to Oregon with their two sons. Since he did not want them to inherit any part of his estate, I made out a will leaving all of his property to the hospital. He died the following year. When the will was presented for probate, his two sons returned from Oregon and employed an attorney in Craig to protest it on the ground that it had been made under excessive pressure. At the trial I was put on the witness chair and asked why Mr. Roland had left all he had to the hospital. I replied that he wanted to save the customary ten-dollar fee I charged for making out a will. At once one of the Roland sons laughed and said, in a voice audible to the jury, "That sounds just like Dad." The jury found in the hospital's favor, and I advanced enough money to the sons for their return trip to Oregon if they would not appeal the judgment.

Now, with all the building costs and facilities paid for, the only remaining matter was to finish the hospital rooms so that the building would be acceptable for patients. The Masonic Lodge offered to buy the furniture for one of the rooms if a plate acknowledging their gift was put on its door. This was followed by similar gifts from the American Legion, the Lion's Club, the Coal Miners Union, and several families requesting memorials for departed members.

Then, after obtaining all the furniture, we looked for a head nurse to run the hospital. As part of my legal work, I had become acquainted with a deputy sheriff in Moffat County, Earl Pate, whose wife was a registered nurse. The two were having a hard time making a living on their homestead, and Mrs. Pate took the position of head nurse at a salary of $150 a month, including bed and board.

Now, it is a peculiar fact that American communities have a genius for building things, but the operation and maintenance of what they have built so cheerfully is another story. Hayden's investment in the J. V. Solandt Memorial Hospital, with provisions for ten beds, came to $35,000. Many residents thought that we had overshot the mark for our needs. Though the building was finished, its practical use still seemed an unattainable goal.

One of our troubles was the usual—our building costs had exceeded our estimates by 150 percent. Simultaneously, hard times had come to Routt County. The cattle market had collapsed, banks had failed, and many of our citizens had lost their homes and savings. The collection of earlier pledges for the hospital was impossible. What we had regarded as Hayden's pride now threatened to become Hayden's white elephant. Some people talked of turning the hospital into a rooming house. Others thought that we might unload it on Routt County for a poorhouse. Nearly all agreed that while a hospital was a good thing, we would be unwise to open it until "times got better."

As the claims against the hospital corporation became more pressing, the directors obtained a loan of $12,000, which was divided into twelve bonds of $1,000 each, secured by a first mortgage on the hospital grounds. Next, the directors made it possible to open the hospital by persuading fifteen Hayden firms, individuals, and several doctors to contribute $10 a month each for running expenses until the hospital began to break even.

Further help came in several ways: the town of Hayden donated the water, the light company gave us six months of electricity, a local coal mine contributed coal, and the telephone company gave us free telephone service for a year. And while it was bad luck for Hayden when the old, established Oxford Hotel burned down, it was a good thing for the hospital because the Bowmans, who ran the hotel, accepted our offer to manage the new institution. Mr. Bowman signed up as janitor at sixty dollars a month, and the hospital's basement rooms supplied ample space for the Bowman's three grandchildren. Mrs. Bowman ran the dining room, boarded the nurses, and provided trays for the patients. We supplied her with all the necessary kitchen utensils and chinaware. We also paid her thirty-five cents for the patients' trays and two dollars a day for boarding the nurses. A volunteer committee of twelve women had charge of the linens.

At last, on April 1, 1923, we were able to open our hospital on a semiregular basis. By then the building was fully equipped for operating, sterilizing, obstetrics, and X-ray, as well as featuring dressing rooms for doctors and two sun parlors.

Our first patient was a twelve-year-old boy who had been sledding downhill and missed a bridge over a ditch at the bottom. He entered the hospital with three broken ribs and a cracked collarbone. The second patient was Bobbie Bower, a popular chuckwagon cook for the Two Bar Cattle Company, who stayed in the hospital for nearly two weeks. So many cowboys came to see him that the place had the appearance of a stockman's hotel.

As the hospital's business manager, I had the task of hiring the nurses and collecting the patients' bills. To reduce the number of unpaid accounts, I instructed Mrs. Pate, the head nurse, never to give a patient a bed until someone responsible had signed a guarantee for the bill—except in emergencies. I did, however, make a few exceptions. One was for Mr. Parfrey, a justice of the peace and retired teacher who ran a small fruit and vegetable store in Hayden. After being discharged from the hospital, he was unable to pay but agreed to collect the hospital's unpaid bills while making partial payments on his own. I turned over to Judge Parfrey $3,000 worth of unpaid accounts. The judge then issued subpoenas to the debtors for the amount of their hospital bills and added his statutory fee of two dollars for issuing the summonses. The debtors, alarmed by the prospect of being hauled into court, rushed to Judge Parfrey asking him to delay their cases. The judge would offer to throw off his subpoena fee and receipt their bills if they paid at once. The savings they gained on the fee induced them to dig up the amount of the hospital bill. The money collected was then turned over to me for the hospital, and I credited Judge Parfrey on his hospital bill with the two-dollar fee that he had thrown off.

Under the supervision of Mrs. Pate, I hired the hospital's nurses. Nonprofessional practical nurses, who were often local housewives seeking to earn some money by doing hospital chores, were not hard to find. But locating registered nurses who were willing to work in our rural district was more difficult. To get help in hiring, I asked the superintendent of the Presbyterian Hospital in Denver to let me present our need to his graduating class of twenty nurses. When I described the J. V. Solandt Memorial Hospital and the joys of rural life, they looked somewhat dubious and asked if there was a movie house in Hayden. I admitted that there was none and immediately was asked, "What do you do for entertainment?" That question was a signal for me to play my trump card. I replied that the reason I had come to Denver looking for nurses was because Routt County was largely populated by handsome young cowboy bachelors and some were prosperous cattlemen. These men, I continued, yearned to end their lonely status and start raising families. When that comment caused a nurse to remark, "Well, I never cared much for movies anyhow," I knew I had a prospect.

Looking back, I think that the four-year period during which our small Hayden community, at great personal sacrifice, pulled together and created the J. V. Solandt Memorial Hospital was a happy one. Though none of us thought much of it at the time, I realize now what a triumph it was for all of us. There was nothing unusual about the way we ran the place, which was open to all doctors. We increased the number of trustees to fifteen—all elected by the stockholders and with Hayden's mayor and district county commissioner serving as ex officio members. The head nurse was in charge, under the authority of the trustees, and the board met once a month (more often if necessary). We had 105 patients the first year, 131 the second and 162 the third. We averaged eighty operative cases during the early years, and about fifteen babies were born there annually, including our daughter Rosamond, born October 25, 1923.

I held the position of secretary of the hospital's board of trustees for the first six or eight years. Every day I tried to visit the hospital to consult with the head nurse and settle administrative problems. I also kept the books and paid the bills. Our methods of charging and collecting were a bit unusual in those early years. We charged a patient twenty-five dollars a week for board, private room, and nursing—the same to every one and with no exceptions. All incoming patients had to deposit one week's charge in advance.

In that remote northwestern corner of Colorado we had almost no charity poor. Social distinctions were nonexistent. The hospital trustees assumed that everyone could pay at a reasonable rate—or if patients themselves could not, then behind them stood first their families, then friends, then lodges or other organizations to which they belonged. As a final resort, of course, there was the county, but we never had to send a bill to Routt County, and Moffat County was asked to pay only two bills. During the first year our collections were 100 percent, while in the second and third years we collected 97.5 percent. No charity work was performed, yet no patient who needed attention was denied it.

We ran an annual deficit of about one hundred dollars a month. After 1923 we took care of this in advance by an annual Hospital Ball. This ball became the big social affair of the year not only for Hayden but for all of Routt and Moffat counties as well. The Hospital Ladies Committee arranged for the music, decorations, and food—all contributed—and the tickets cost fifty cents. So great was the response that we netted nearly $1,200 in the first year and well over that amount in later years.

One of America's great philosophers, William James, said that we would never be able to do without war until we found its "moral equivalent"—something evoking the same amount of courage, hard work, sacrifice, and cooperation. As a way of putting to a test a community's courage and stamina, I recommend opening a hospital in a small town like Hayden. The challenges are constant and seemingly insurmountable. There never seems to be enough money to make ends meet. Two patients may be there one day and seventeen the next. Extra practical nurses may suddenly have imperative duties cleaning house or canning peaches, and the head nurse and a cook may fail to agree on their respective stations in the hospital's hierarchy—a problem that one doctor told me could only be solved by the rule "Head nurses are easier to come by than good cooks." Furthermore, a surgeon may refuse at a critical point to operate unless a favorite nurse is there to assist, or a lady visitor may spy dirt under the radiators and tell all the gossips in town that the place is in filthy condition. The trustees have to find time from their proper business of earning a living to resolve these problems that threaten the usefulness of the institution.

Those who go abroad may notice that the most striking feature of European small towns is a cathedral situated on an over-

TOP LEFT: *Mrs. Emma H. Peck, longtime county superintendent of schools.* TOP RIGHT: *Farrington and Eunice in front of the new Hayden Union High School, January 1921.* CENTER: *Hayden Boy Rangers with their leader in front of the Hayden School, about 1922.* BOTTOM: *Solandt Memorial Hospital in Hayden, about 1929. With sixteen beds, it was the only accredited hospital between Denver and Salt Lake City.*

looking hill. A relic of the Middle Ages, the cathedral represents the aspirations of the community for the good and the beautiful. In Colorado's small towns those buildings that stand for the same aspirations are community projects like our J. V. Solandt Memorial Hospital.

When the Hayden community saw in 1919 that its dream of a hospital would be realized, its leaders were inspired to push other plans for the well-being of our townspeople young and old. Seven bonds were voted in 1919 to finance a waterworks, a sewer system, and an improved Routt County fairground. Most important of all, bonds were issued on September 1, 1919, for the Hayden Union High School building.

I had been on the board of the Elkhead School since 1915. When I returned from the army, I was put on the District Two school board in Hayden. My aim was to secure consolidation of several districts into a single modern high school. In Routt County public schools through the eighth grade were to be found in forty-four school districts. Some districts were so small that they had only one resident family with children of school age. Others were so large that several schoolhouses had to be provided for a widely scattered population. The only high schools in Routt County were in the towns of Yampa, Oak Creek, Steamboat Springs, and Hayden. Students from other districts had to pay tuition to attend high school.

Mrs. Emma H. Peck of Hayden had been elected school superintendent of Routt County, and her husband, Harry Peck, was county assessor. Both had held office for so many years that nobody could remember their predecessors. They had four children, three sons and a daughter. She referred to them as "a bushel of kids—the four Pecks." Her duties were to call elections for new districts, examine and license teachers, prescribe courses of study, attend graduating exercises, hand out diplomas, and renew her acquaintance with parents and friends who supported her politically.

Mrs. Peck deplored the fact that a public high school education was not free to our rural students. She decided to take advantage of a law allowing school districts to consolidate into a union high school. Six districts in the neighborhood of Hayden's were invited to vote themselves into a single Union High School District. I went along with Mrs. Peck at meetings to urge representatives from the six districts to join the Union district. The Hayden district responded to Mrs. Peck's idea by voting a bond issue which gave the town enough money for a fine, modern high school building with a large gymnasium, assembly room, swimming pool, shower room, manual training and domestic science rooms, laboratories, a school library, and a reading room.

I was elected chairman of the Hayden District Board of Education. Our first task was to find a superintendent who would select a faculty to carry out the high standards that the Hayden community expected of their new school. We had heard praise of a high school superintendent in Illinois named Charles A. Stoddard, and I asked my sister, Ruth Woodley, in Evanston to call on him. He impressed her favorably and we gave him a five-year contract as superintendent of Hayden Union High School at a salary of $2,500 for the first year and $500 more a year in the next four. While serving for six years as our superintendent, Stoddard filed on a 640-acre stock-raising homestead three miles from Oak Point. When he resigned he sold this land and purchased the *Empire-Courier*, a weekly newspaper in Craig. Though he never ran for public office, he was influential all his life in the councils of Colorado's Republican party.

NINE

Crickets and the "Moffat Tunnel Steal"

The election in 1920 of Republican Warren G. Harding as president ended a decade of Democratic control in Routt County and placed three Republican members on the new Board of County Commissioners. Since I was precinct chairman of the Republican party in the Hayden district, I was appointed county attorney at an annual salary of $850. The position allowed me to continue my private law practice and gave me an excellent chance to become familiar with county government.

In those days the county courthouse provided office space for county officials, a courtroom for trials, and a jail. Wherever the courthouse was located became the county seat. By tradition it had to be within a day's journey by horseback for every county resident. Routt County had had three county seats—first Hayden, then Hahn's Peak, and finally Steamboat Springs, whose modern brick building was the ornament of the town.

County commissioners then were usually middle-aged men who, having been successful in their private affairs, were willing to work part-time at a modest stipend supervising county government. The office was—and is—a prestigious one in most communities. The commissioners who appointed me Routt County attorney in 1920 were Alva Jones, Amos A. Chivington, and A. H. Poppen. Jones, a Republican from the Hayden district who also served on the Hayden town council, was the owner of the town's livery barn. When it came to horse trading he was considered a real Yankee. Chivington, who was from the Yampa district, had been the county sheriff for eight years. A great vote-getter and greeter, he was familiarly called "Old Snort" because he made a peculiar nasal sound when he talked. Poppen was a semiretired banker from the Steamboat Springs district. His frugality was publicized by a few words painted on a signpost at the end of town—"Jesus Saves." To this the town jokers had added: "So does Poppen."

Once a month I drove to Steamboat Springs with Commissioner Jones and spent several days there during the commissioners' regular meetings. To save hotel expenses, we all slept in the jury room of the courthouse, where cots, mattresses, and bedding had been stored for the jurors to use when court was in session. Regardless of political affiliation, county officers who had served several terms together often developed a fraternal spirit, and this group came to be called the "Courthouse Gang."

The meetings were conducted informally, and anyone was allowed to attend and take part in the discussions. Much of the commissioners' time was involved in routine duties such as auditing and approving salaries, wages, and purchased materials. Welfare matters were handled through a special levy called the Poor Fund. The board had wide discretion in using money from that fund and spent a good deal of time discussing it.

At one meeting, a young widow whose husband had been killed in a coal mine came before the commissioners asking for support. She was carrying a baby in her arms, and two small youngsters were holding on to her skirt. When she left the room, Commissioner Poppen said that although the woman had no means of support, she had gained a reputation for being extravagant. After long debate the commissioners assigned her an allowance of $27.50 a month.

At the next meeting Commissioner Poppen announced that the widow had spent all of her allowance on sugar cookies and canned pineapple. He also reported that he had been forced to buy the woman oatmeal and other staple foods to last her the rest of the month. Later, as the commissioners were looking over the Poor Fund bills, Poppen's face suddenly turned red. Throwing a bill on the table, he exclaimed, "If we pay *that*, I'll resign from this board." The bill had been sent from the largest store in Steamboat Springs for two pair of silk stockings, a silk brassiere, and two silk panties purchased by the widow. The other commis-

TOP LEFT: *Pioneer cattleman John Charles Temple.* TOP RIGHT: *Routt County Commissioner Alva Jones.* RIGHT: *J. N. ("Jap") Wyman, Morapos Creek pioneer.*

sioners looked at it without comment. Near the close of the session, Commissioner Jones returned to it and picked it up.

"I think this bill should be paid," he said, "and I'll tell you why. Last month I needed a new grader blade for one of my road men. When I went to Steamboat to get it from the road supervisor, I found him at the Legion Hall dancing with the widow and holding her very close. Now, if we can just keep her in silk panties for a few more weeks, I don't believe we'll have her on our hands much longer." The bill was paid, and sure enough the road supervisor and the widow were married that fall.

Another strategem used to reduce the strain on the Poor Fund was to send one Routt County welfare recipient to the milder climate of Grand Junction for the winter. Thus, for the cost of travel expense alone, the commissioners managed to get Mesa County to support the man for six months out of the year. In another case, Commissioner Alva Jones and I visited an old man living near Hahn's Peak who had been drawing fifteen dollars a month from the Poor Fund for some time. When we got to his cabin, we noticed rabbit hides tacked on the wall. Commissioner Jones asked the man what he did with the rabbits after he skinned them.

"I get twenty-five cents each for their carcasses," he replied. "If the county furnished me with shells for my rifle, I'd get enough rabbits to live all right and wouldn't need your relief money." Commissioner Jones pondered the proposal momentarily and then said: "Can you use .22 shorts?" The cheapest .22 ammunition available, shorts were used mainly for target practice. But the old man, proud of his skill with a rifle, assured the commissioner that "shorts" would be fine. The deal was struck and the county was relieved of fifteen dollars a month expense from the Poor Fund less the cost of the cheaper shells.

Commissioner Jones saved the county even more money in the case of a bed invalid who was in the care of a widow in Hayden. She had complained to the commissioners that the man was incontinent and her laundry costs were more than the county was paying for his keep. Jones advised her to stop using linen sheets and to substitute unsold copies of *The Denver Post* that she could get for free from the Hayden drugstore.

The problems of the poor, however, were by no means the only matters of concern for the county commissioners. During World War I, for instance, the railroads had been under federal control and as such were released from paying property taxes. After the war, when the railroads were returned to private ownership, the receiver for the Moffat Road proposed to settle with each of the nine counties through which the railroad ran, by offering to pay the principal amount but none of the interest and penalties that had accrued during the war years. When this settlement was offered to Routt County, I advised the Board of County Commissioners that the railroad was indeed liable for interest and penalties. Moffat County then joined Routt County in a suit to collect the full amount, and I was chosen to represent both counties. In an opinion written by Colorado Supreme Court Justice Haslett P. Burke, the two counties were awarded both interest and penalties. For my fee in that case I charged the two counties a total of $2,000, which was the largest I had ever earned. I had promised Eunice that I would give the fee to her, and with the money she purchased a Steinway grand piano that became the family gathering point thereafter for singing cowboy songs and Christmas carols.

By far the most dramatic event of my eight-year term as county attorney was the terrible "cricket war" that took place in Routt and Moffat counties during the summers of 1927 and 1928. Moving like a great army across the land, hordes of these insects—which we called "Mormon crickets" because they arrived from Utah—first came to our attention when they struck Brown's Park a hundred miles to the west of Hayden. The alarm of the Hayden community, as well as my own, grew rapidly as the crickets crossed the Routt-Moffat county line and began laying eggs in Breeze Basin not far from the wheat fields of the Dawson Ranch.

What drew this insect army eastward along the Yampa River from Utah were irrigated fields of wheat and oats that had begun to be developed in World War I when high prices were paid for grain crops. Unable to survive on the brush and juniper of the arid plains and mesas of eastern Utah and northwestern Colorado, the crickets were naturally attracted to these new fields. Actually "Mormon crickets" were large, dark katydids which had long antennae and legs built for leaping thirty to forty feet at a time. As their short legs cracked together they made a sharp chirping noise that in concert could be heard some distance away. In their search for food they had developed an aggressive-

Litigation over the newly completed Moffat Tunnel, states Farrington Carpenter, "brought me the nickname 'Dynamite Carpenter' and gave me a . . . reputation as a maverick." He called it the "Moffat Tunnel steal."

ness and a skill at mass movement that made them the most feared insects in the Rocky Mountain region. They were omnivorous and cannibalistic, attacking animal flesh as well as crops. Even worse, before each female cricket died, it laid about two hundred eggs in the ground—and we knew that when all those eggs hatched in the spring, a new and much larger cricket army would drive eastward like its ancestors, eating everything in sight.

When we first heard the sound of the crickets in Routt County I was called to a meeting in Hayden by Commissioner Jones, Chivington, and Poppen to plan a course of action. Our first scheme, as suggested by old-timers, was to scare the oncoming marauders with noise. Hundreds of farmers around Hayden protected their gardens or small fields night and day by ringing bells, blowing horns, pounding on tin buckets, or rattling tin cans on a wire. To avoid the hubbub the crickets first passed around their property, but the noise failed to stop the main body of the invading army. We therefore appealed for advice to the State Agricultural College at Fort Collins, whose experts recommended spraying the crickets with arsenic and ground lime. The college also sent two young men with a great quantity of this spray, which they dispensed through spray guns carried on foot and on horseback or mounted on the hoods of Model-T Fords. Unfortunately the crickets seemed to thrive on this spray, and the more treatment they received the better they ate and the more active they became.

In sympathy with our plight, friends at the Livestock Exchange in Denver sent us a carload of turkeys to gobble up the crickets, and the Moffat Road delivered the turkeys in a freight car free of charge. When the gobblers were finally turned loose in our fields, a mad race began as they ran in every direction to catch crickets. After half an hour, however, the turkeys lost their appetite and many of them got sick from the arsenic spray. As soon as one would lie down, crickets would swarm all over it and begin eating it alive.

So the crickets thwarted our every move. If a tree stood in their way they would get to the top of it in one mighty leap. If they got into a house they would devour everything inside. With all the season's grain in danger of destruction, we were desperate.

Through trial and error, however, we had discovered that a vertical tin fence fifteen inches high and three inches into the ground would stop most of the crickets—and it so happened that the county commissioners had just purchased four miles of tin sheeting to use in road work and the construction of bridges and culverts. It was just what we needed. We decided to stretch a fence for two and a half miles on the ridge between the Yampa River and Williams Fork to the south. Yet we soon realized that we had a few things to learn. For one thing, the tin fence had to be nailed to wood stakes, but if the stakes were on the side facing the crickets the pests crawled right up the stakes and over the fence. Thus we had to lean the tin a little bit towards the arriving army, and when they could not get over the fifteen-inch fence the crickets would flop along the side. About every one hundred feet we also built a pit two feet deep and four feet square lined with tin so that crickets which fell inside could not crawl out again. In fact, all of us had some fun outsmarting the crickets, and to support the hundreds of volunteer cricket fighters the ranch and farm wives organized picnics with huge campfires where coffee and sandwiches were served throughout the night.

In a few days, as the main body of the cricket army reached the tin fence, the pits filled up with insects. Squads of men and boys poured gasoline on them and did away with billions of crickets. Some of us stood by, our shovels ready for any that escaped the pits. Once a big rattlesnake fell into a pit and squirmed around with crickets devouring him. Soon there was nothing but a snake skeleton left.

After three weeks of this battle, the remaining crickets began laying their eggs. In the following spring the hatchings were only the size of a housefly and the birds ate them up. Later, entomologists told us that what really finished off the crickets was a parasite insect that laid its eggs inside the cricket eggs and destroyed the hatch, saving Routt County from more crop destruction.

All of us in the Hayden community congratulated ourselves on winning our 1927–28 cricket war at a total cost of $4,655.79. That sum was spent for two tons of poison, spray guns, haulage, and ten miles of tin. Much of the cost was donated by Hayden merchants and civic bodies, with Routt County making up the difference.

At the end of my service as Routt County attorney, I decided in 1928 to run for district attorney. The county job had become routine, my civil law practice was small, the Dawson Ranch ensured my living and a bit more, and I felt that a fellow should try something new every four years of his life to keep his humility pump greased up. The office of the district attorney for the Fourteenth Judicial District included Routt, Moffat, and Grand counties. It paid $3,000 a year and included a stenographer as well as an assistant to handle minor legal matters.

I distributed a campaign brochure featuring a picture of me all slicked up and wearing a white shirt, a coat, and a tie. I also attended a banquet of pioneers in Granby with Eunice, put my posters everywhere, spoke at the colored church in Mount Harris, and got the support of the old-time cowmen and sheephaters. All our campaigning must have counted because I was elected district attorney easily.

My first big criminal case occurred in 1929–30. Elmer Stephenson, a Yampa resident, had collapsed and died one day after drinking a cup of coffee served by his wife, Lillian. Elmer's friends in Yampa spread the rumor that Mrs. Stephenson had put strychnine in his coffee. According to the rumor, after her husband's death she planned to collect on his $3,500 life insurance policy—which had been issued a week before he died—and then to marry her boyfriend, who lived in Mancos.

Mrs. Stephenson asked me as an official to do something to stop the rumors. She brought me what she said was a suicide note written by Mr. Stephenson asserting his love for his wife. I called in handwriting experts from New York City and Chicago who declared that the suicide note was a forgery.

The trial drew a large audience and Lillian Stephenson was the center of attraction. She sported a new hairdo and wore a lowcut, tight-fitting velvet dress over her fulsome figure. The male jurors could not keep their eyes from her. Whenever their attention strayed, she would lean forward and pour out a glass of ice water, sipping this for some minutes just as I was trying to make an important point—such as the difference between murder and manslaughter—to the ogling jurors.

No evidence was found to indicate where Mrs. Stephenson might have gotten the strychnine and the judge did not permit me to show that is was a common poison found in every rancher's house to use against coyotes. After deliberating for forty-eight hours the jury brought in a verdict of not guilty. Mrs. Stephenson collected the life insurance money, moved to Mancos, and married John Rundell. Throughout the trial he had been referred to as the "mattress man" because evidence at the trial disclosed that when Stephenson came home early from work one day he found Rundell hidden under a mattress.

I was sorry to lose the Lillian Stephenson case but something far more important soon came my way that brought me the nickname "Dynamite Carpenter" and gave me a statewide reputation as a maverick. It was a piece of litigation that attracted national interest—one I called the "Moffat Tunnel steal."

For years the growth of the city and county of Denver had been curtailed by both a shortage of water and the failure of the Moffat Road to push its line beyond Craig to Salt Lake City. In 1922 the Colorado legislature responded with the Moffat Tunnel Act, which provided for the building of a 6.4-mile tunnel under James Peak that would carry Western Slope water to Denver (by means of the adjoining pioneer bore) as well as Moffat Road trains. The tunnel would permit trains to cross the Continental Divide at a point 2,400 feet lower than the older, spectacularly high passage over Corona Pass. It would reduce the distance of the crossing by twenty-three miles, thus fulfilling David Moffat's dream of a railroad "Gateway to the West" for Denver.

While the Moffat Tunnel—the world's fourth longest—was being built, a new company called the Denver and Salt Lake Railway appeared in 1925. Supplanting the Denver and Salt Lake Rail*road* (the original Moffat Road), it was created by a syndicate formed by three of the most powerful men in Colorado: Gerald Hughes, a wealthy Denver attorney; Lawrence Phipps, who was then Colorado's senior senator; and the multimillionaire Charles Boettcher, owner of the Ideal Cement Company.

The Denver and Salt Lake Railway Company obtained permission from the Interstate Commerce Commission to buy the old Moffat Road, which had gone bankrupt, out of receivership. Plans were soon made to build a short railroad spur between the D&SL line at Bond, Colorado, and the line of the Denver and Rio Grande at Dotsero. Since the D&RG line already connected with Salt Lake City, this forty-one-mile Dotsero Cutoff would give Denver its gateway to the west but would leave our Moffat Road permanently stalled at Craig. In addition, with the cutoff route a distinct possibility and costs for the still-incomplete Moffat Tunnel going ever higher, the syndicate was in a position to garner a handsome profit while the taxpayers of Routt, Moffat, Grand, and other counties along the Moffat Road lost potential revenue.

In January 1926 the syndicate contracted with the Moffat Tunnel Commission, which controlled the financing and use of the tunnel, for a ninety-nine-year lease. However, it was not until 1928, when the D&SL trains were using the tunnel regularly and the tracks over Corona Pass had been abandoned, that I had a chance to read that contract. I saw immediately that the lease violated two major provisions of the Moffat Tunnel Act of 1922— one part of which prohibited monopolistic use of the tunnel and another relating to the responsibility of the users to pay interest on the bonds as well as a portion of the amount necessary to retire them.

It seemed inconceivable to me that such a blatant evasion of legal requirements could have been overlooked for nearly three years. When I tried to get someone in Denver to question the document, I found no one willing to make war on the powerful syndicate. However, a Moffat County friend and former sheriff, Joseph J. Jones, let me use his name as plaintiff. On January 8, 1929, in the District Court of Moffat County in Craig, I filed for an injunction to stop the parties from using the tunnel under a contract collusively and fraudulently obtained.

This case, *J. J. Jones v. the Moffat Tunnel Commission*, set off a furor. *The Denver Post* supported our suit and came out with a favorable front-page cartoon showing J. J. Jones about to rope a mad bull labeled "The Moffat Tunnel Commission." Meanwhile, during the same month, the tunnel commission began a suit in federal court to hold the railroad to the terms of the Moffat Tunnel Act, while the syndicate returned with its own suit to uphold its lease on the tunnel.

In April the syndicate, on a motion granted by the state court, removed our case to the federal district court in Denver, which by this time had decided in favor of the railroad. Now the tunnel commission and the syndicate ignored any further charges of illegality of the contract for lease and use as a whole and collusion between the contracting parties. Since the case had already been tried in the federal court, I was reduced to what I could present in the circuit court of appeals—to which the tunnel commission had appealed the case. So I filed a brief asking for the right to appear for J. J. Jones as *amicus curiae*, or friend of the court. The city of

Denver and several other parties also filed *amicus* briefs. All of us asked the court to invalidate the Moffat Tunnel lease.

On November 24, 1930, the arguments were heard. The courtroom was packed with lawyers, reporters, and spectators. Three federal judges presided in somber splendor. I was the last to be called upon to present my objections to the decision of the district court affirming the legality of the lease. As I gathered my pages of notes and stood up to speak, a whispered conversation took place among the judges. Judge Lewis, who was presiding, cleared his throat and said: "Mr. Carpenter, this court will not listen to any charges of fraud or collusion in the making of the contract and lease under consideration today. There is nothing in the record to support such charges, and you may not refer to them."

I was dumbfounded. I cited a United States Supreme Court case holding that the question of fraud could be raised at any time in the proceedings, even after execution had issued. The court was unimpressed.

I did not have the nerve to defy the appeals court. If it had sentenced me to jail for contempt, I am certain a public reaction would have resulted, perhaps bringing a more correct conclusion to the case. As it turned out, it upheld the district court, and the United States Supreme Court upheld the appeals court. I had learned equity from Roscoe Pound at Harvard and common-law pleading from Dean Ames, but I was a young fellow who got trimmed out in the Colorado court. My failure to stand up to the court of appeals I consider to have been one of the worst errors of my life.

In the history of the development of the West, this "Moffat Tunnel steal" stands out as a classic example of misdirected legislative prodigality, administrative ineptitude, inflexibility of court procedure, and robber-baron cupidity.

With the Moffat Tunnel case behind me, I gave a paper on county government to the Colorado Bar Association convention in Colorado Springs. In that paper I stated:

> Progress in Colorado is being blocked because the distribution of tax funds is in the hands of local officials—county commissioners and school directors. Both are handicapped by an outworn system. It is easy to see why local government is so costly. There are twenty counties in Colorado with less

than five thousand population each and three counties with only a thousand people in them. How can such small counties afford the cost of a complete county government? Colorado started off with seventeen counties instead of today's sixty-three. Elimination of the cost of forty-six county governments would save the taxpayers millions of dollars a year.

Although the paper was published in several newspapers it aroused too little public interest to cause any legislative action. I decided that the initiative for tax relief was within the powers of the Board of County Commissioners, which could bring about reforms without the need for state legislation to authorize them. Soon the opportunity to work for reform as a commissioner arose when Commissioner R. I. Gwillim of Oak Creek offered to work with me if I could get elected as such.

By doing that, however, I would be violating one of the most respected rules of politics—never to abandon an office of greater prestige and salary for one of less. As Routt County commissioner I would get only $850 a year and no secretarial help. This was a negation of the usual practice of always trying to ascend in the political hierarchy and not slipping in the opposite direction. Nevertheless, I declined renomination for district attorney in the fall of 1931 and announced my candidacy for Routt County commissioner.

Republican party captains advised against my course of action and refused to give my candidacy any party support. And although I had no trouble getting the nomination, I thereafter found I was a "loner"—uninvited to the party's caucuses and public meetings. That treatment, however, was just the challenge I needed to go all out and campaign for myself. Advertising a schedule of public meetings in schoolhouses all over the county I got Charley Stoddard and Ralph White from Craig and a third barbershop singer to provide musical entertainment. We advertised them as the "Sagebrush Orioles."

I also employed a public accountant from Denver to scrutinize all bills that Routt County had paid in the past year. Many of these had not been notarized and for that reason were illegal. So I asked the county engineer to make a large map depicting in black all the quarter sections that were in tax default. (In those days of depression this included most of the ranches and farmhouses in Routt County.) I then demonstrated what I considered to be a dangerous state of affairs in Routt County government.

My opponent in that race was a neighboring rancher and friend, Henry Summers, who owned and operated the only butcher shop in Hayden. He came from a pioneer family and was widely known and liked. His two sons were in my Junior Boy Scout organization and his only daughter, Marie, was a nurse at Solandt Memorial Hospital.

The five women who constituted the Hayden Business Women's Club decided to hold a public meeting at which candidates from both parties could speak. Since Summers was not a public speaker, I thought it a bit unfair that we had been pitted against each other in debate. After sixteen years as a trial lawyer, I was at home speaking on my feet.

At the meeting, after I had related all the shortcomings and extravagances of the present Board of County Commissioners, Summers was called upon. He came forward smiling and said, "Well, folks, you've heard what Ferry says he'll do to cut costs if he's elected, and I think he's right—they need cutting. I've been your butcher for many years and you *know* how I trim the fat and bone off your meat cuts, so maybe I can do as well with county expenses." That was all he said, but Henry's remarks brought laughter and loud applause—and later, votes.

When the ballots had all been counted, Henry was elected by a narrow margin and I was defeated. For the first time in twelve years I was without a paid political office. The lesson it taught me was that there are more voters interested in how public money is spent than how it can be saved.

TEN

Keep out the Sheep!

City dwellers often ask me how we survived the monotony of life in isolated mountain regions like Routt and Moffat counties. I can tell them that life in Hayden, Colorado, was anything but dull during the Roaring Twenties—with the cricket invasion, the Stephenson murder trial, and the Moffat Tunnel Steal. And then, of course, at the start of the 1920s came the bitter battle between the cattlemen and the sheepmen.

The issues of that battle had been building for more than a decade. It was not because either group was composed of bad men longing to murder one another for misdeeds, for those misdeeds were acts of happenstance brought on by the influx of homesteaders taking up land in northwestern Colorado, where usable land was already in short supply.

I noticed this shortage in our two counties around 1906, when President Theodore Roosevelt withdrew Routt National Forest and White River National Forest from homestead entry. The vast, windy sagebrush region of Moffat County, running one hundred miles from Craig to Utah, was unclaimed federal grazing land that the big Colorado cattle companies used free of charge. Homesteading on these federal grazing lands was not practical until 1916, when Congress created the 640-acre, free, stock-raising homestead. Hundreds of "dry land" homesteaders flocked to, filed on, and fenced most of the water holes of Moffat County. That threatened the big cattle companies, which needed both the unfenced open range and scarce water to stay in business.

At the time, I was retained as attorney for the Hayden Cattle-men's Association and other cow groups in Routt and Moffat counties. I advised my clients to take advantage of federal law allowing them to file on stock-raising watering places. A cattleman could file on forty acres with a spring; the government would withdraw those forty acres from entry; and no homesteader could file on them.

I also argued civil and criminal law cases for the cattlemen's associations. The influx of land-hungry people attracted many dishonest operators as well as honest people who were pushed to bankruptcy when they found it impossible to make a living on the sagebrush lands they had homesteaded. With all those open-range cattle running loose in Moffat County, rustlers would butcher a range steer and sell the meat to company stores in the coal mine towns.

Then, as my historian friend, John Rolfe Burroughs of Steam-boat Springs, has written in his classic history of northwestern Colorado, *Where the Old West Stayed Young*, around 1911 the big cattlemen began to complain of a new threat to their free open range—flocks of sheep coming into Moffat County from Utah. As the cattlemen saw it, their open range ought to be kept sacro-sanct for cattle. For one thing, sheep grazed the scarce grass a little closer than cattle, and for another, cattle always ran free. Thus a sheepherder and his dogs could hold the sheep near a water hole and the cattle, hesitant to come near, would drift to another range. So the cattlemen told the sheepmen to stay out of their range as far as the Utah line to the west and the Wyoming line to the north. They also employed riders to patrol those state lines daily, and if sheepmen trespassed, a committee of cattlemen told them to take their sheep back to Utah.

Usually the sheepmen obeyed, but if not, trouble followed—as occurred in December 1911, when five cowmen with clubs and knives killed 110 head of sheep on the George Woolley place southeast of Craig. The sheepmen took that warning to heart and kept out of the way of the cattlemen until April 1920, when seven armed and masked men took two young sheepherders from the Keeley homestead in the northeastern corner of Rio Blanco County, which adjoins Moffat County. Having bound and gagged the two herders, the masked men clubbed their entire band of 350 sheep to death. Snellen Johnson, the Utah owner of the sheep, tried to have the seven masked men arrested but was told by the district attorney that a conviction was impossible to obtain in northwestern Colorado, where juries were dominated by the cattle barons.

After the Keeley affair, sheep-hating cattlemen behaved themselves for a few weeks. Then on July 30, 1920, a posse of eleven cattlemen called on a sheepherder named Darnell, whose flock had crossed into Moffat County four miles from the Utah line. When the herder, sleeping in his sheep wagon, heard the intruders and fired two warning shots, they sprayed him with bullets. After this murder, they clubbed 686 of Darnell's flock of 1,800 sheep to death. This extreme act of violence attracted the attention of the federal government. As cited in Burroughs's book, the *Craig Empire Courier* of December 22, 1920, told the ensuing story in its headlines:

> U. S. Arrests Six to End Sheep War. After Months of Investigation, Prominent Northwestern Colorado Cattlemen Are Indicted by Federal Grand Jury. Accused of Attempting Fraud. Intimidating Homesteaders Charged, and Government Attorney Will Prosecute to the Limit.

The federal agents had no better luck prosecuting the indicted cattlemen than had the district attorney the previous April. Then, just as the furor of the sheep-cattle war had begun to subside, many cattlemen, suffering from low cattle prices, were unable to pay for their grazing pemits in the White River National Forest south of Craig, and these were purchased by Utah sheepmen. This setback was followed by the election of Warren G. Harding as president of the United States, and Harding appointed as secretary of the interior Albert B. Fall, a former senator from New Mexico. Thereafter Fall named as commissioner of the General Land Office, which managed the federal grazing lands of northwestern Colorado, former governor William Spry of Utah.

Spry, of course, was a sheepman and very friendly with the Utah sheep owners, who, together with Spry declared a stock driveway for the sheep from Utah to their new grazing allotments in the White River National Forest. The stock driveway, which was 106 miles long and 6 miles wide with resting places about every 25 miles, was a tremendous boon to the Utah sheepmen. Before Commissioner Spry set it up, the sheepmen had been forced to ship their animals by rail from eastern Utah on the D&RG to Denver, then west again on the Moffat Road to the little town of Yampa, where they could be trailed a dozen miles to the White River National Forest.

From the Colorado cattlemen's point of view, the stock driveway could not be allowed because it passed through the best of their open-range cattle country. They pointed out that during the several weeks of passage to the White River National Forest along the 106-mile driveway, the sheep would eat off much of the grass that the cattlemen needed for their huge cowherds. As attorney for the cattlemen, I passed along their views to the Utah sheepmen, who nevertheless decided to make a test case of the driveway. When two bands of their sheep reached the little settlement of Sunbeam on the Yampa River in Moffat County's rolling sage country, the sheepmen sent word to Governor Oliver Shoup of Colorado asking for the state militia to protect their sheep from the angry cattlemen.

Governor Shoup did not order out the militia, but he did send a carload of Colorado state police and two motorcycle patrolmen. They posted themselves at the Moffat County courthouse in Craig, where the cattlemen were holding a protest meeting just as the two bands of sheep from Sunbeam passed through and headed south on the stock driveway, convoyed by six uniformed state police trailing a mounted gatling gun.

I knew the road through which the stock driveway passed almost by heart, having hunted bobcats along it with my friend J. N. ("Jap") Wyman. The cattle associations were pressing me to find some way to stop the sheep on the driveway, but I realized that as long as the sheep stayed on public roads and on that part of the public domain constituting the driveway, there was no legal way to turn them back. However, I recalled that shortly after the driveway crossed from Moffat County into Rio Blanco County the road ran along Morapos Creek below Thornburgh Mountain—and the land on both sides of that road was owned by the selfsame Jap Wyman.

Under Colorado law, county commissioners had the power to abandon a county road on behalf of whoever owned the lands bordering it. We had to move fast by telephone because the sheep were only ten miles or so from Wyman's ranch. The three Rio Blanco county commissioners were loyal cattlemen, and when Wyman petitioned them to abandon the road through his ranch, they met in an emergency session.

I waited tensely with a mob of armed cowboys at the Wyman ranch house as the two Utah sheep owners, their herders, and the sheep approached the ranch preceded by the state police. At 2:00 P.M. Wyman's phone rang. I grabbed it, and the Rio Blanco commissioners told me that they had just signed the order abandoning the county road. The cowboys rushed forward with a roll of hog wire and built a fence across it. I explained to the baffled state police captain what had happened—that the road was now private property and no sheep or their owners could trespass on it without a warrant. When the Utah sheep owners arrived, I suggested that the best thing they could do was to take their sheep back to Craig and put them on the freight cars of the Moffat Road to get them to Yampa and the national forest. As Burroughs has noted, the presence of the state police prevented any fights, although one cattleman broke a bone in his instep while kicking a sheep that had wandered onto his premises.

All in all, testing the legality of the stock driveway had been a costly experiment to the Utah sheep owners, who subsequently admitted that it had all but ruined them financially.

For the time being, we had kept the sheep out of northwestern Colorado, but all of us knew that the only real solution was to have the sheep driveway revoked by the Department of the Interior and Commissioner Spry. To this end the cattlemen appealed to Colorado's senators, Lawrence C. Phipps and Samuel D. Nicholson, to arrange for a hearing in Washington with a committee of cattlemen to present the local point of view to the commissioner. Nine associations of cattlemen from northwestern Colorado and one from Wyoming elected a committee headed by old-time Hayden cattleman Charles Temple, who was chairman of the Northwest Colorado Stockgrowers' Federation. I was put on the committee with Joe Neal, a banker from Meeker, and "Uncle Joe" Reef, one of our region's most colorful men. Uncle Joe, as everyone addressed him, had brought his money out from Illinois in the 1880s and had become a leading Moffat County cattle baron. He owned a good deal of Denver real estate and a meat packing plant in Pueblo. Seventy-two years old in 1922, powerfully built, over six feet tall, and with a florid face and a shock of white hair, Uncle Joe never asserted himself, but such was his charm that he was always the center of attention.

Before the four of us got to Washington for the hearing, I prepared our complaint about the stock driveway for Senator Phipps. I explained that there was a good sheep trail from Yampa to the White River National Forest and that the sheepmen should ship their animals by rail to that point and use their own trail. I stated that Commissioner Spry, who had created the stock driveway without consulting anyone, was prejudiced in favor of the Utah sheepmen. I also argued that the Routt and Moffat county grazing range had been available for the cattlemens' exclusive use since the early settlement of Brown's Park in the 1850s. It was plainly wrong to allow the itinerant sheep entry by way of the driveway. The Utah sheep owners did not live in our counties, owned no land in our counties, paid no taxes to speak of in our counties, and we regarded them as trespassers. To prove my point, I drew up a table of the relative importance of the livestock industries in northwestern Colorado showing a total of 4,326 resident cattle owners, as compared with 24 resident sheep owners. Our cattle were valued at $3,376,430 compared with sheep worth $236,553.

In a second complaint for Secretary Fall, I declared for the cattlemen that the sheep driveway had the effect of splitting Moffat County in the middle. It was a region occupied by homesteaders and small ranchers whose principal product was hay, which they sold to the cattlemen, who bought 65,000 tons annually. On the other hand, the sheepmen bought only 200 tons a year. The hay on the driveway grew on a loose formation of native soil which could not withstand sheep grazing for more than two seasons before the grass would die out and the weeds take over. My complaint added:

> In recent years, large bands of tramp sheep have invaded Colorado from Utah. Their owners belong to no associations and make and keep no agreements. To them the Moffat County grazing area is free range and is theirs for the taking. In some cases, they have hired or grubstaked Colorado ranch men to run Utah sheep as their own.

The Colorado homesteader found that barbed wire did not

protect his hay from the foreign sheep which grazed right under the bottom of the wire. The sheepherders, who were largely Mexican, left no money in Moffat County, bringing in from Utah all they needed to stock their sheep wagons.

On our arrival in Washington, the two Colorado senators escorted us to the Department of the Interior, where Secretary Fall presided at the hearing. He was surrounded by a covey of aides and lawyers, which included Commissioner Spry. The members of our committee displayed a large map of northwestern Colorado showing that the economic well-being of the area was entirely sustained by property taxes paid by residents who were all in the cattle business.

Very few questions about the stock driveway were asked of us. In my statement I merely said: "Colorado cattlemen have no objection to adequate grazing by Colorado sheep, but the citizens of the region are unanimous in their opposition to allowing Utah sheep to travel many miles into the interior of Colorado to reach grazing ground in White River National Forest which can be reached by rail." I stopped there as it was quite evident to me that the officials wanted to hear from Uncle Joe Reef.

When I finished, Secretary Fall turned to Uncle Joe and asked him if he thought sheep and cattle could get along amicably on the same range.

"If you ever smelled of a sheep bed-ground," Uncle Joe replied, "you would not need to ask that question."

The secretary then asked Uncle Joe if this was his first visit to the nation's capital.

"No," said Uncle Joe. "The first time I was here was when I marched as a private in the victorious Army of the Potomac in a parade down Pennsylvania Avenue. I saluted President Johnson and Secretary of War Stanton on the receiving stand in front of the White House. All the flags were at half-mast because of the recent assassination of President Lincoln."

A hush fell on the hearing room as Uncle Joe finished speaking. It was only broken when Secretary Fall invited him to go to the White House and meet President Harding. The secretary then adjourned the hearing. After the cattlemen met in a back room for a brief conference with our two senators, word came from Secretary Fall that the stock driveway would be rescinded and the sheepmen on it would be allowed thirty days to remove their sheep.

Charley Temple and I rushed to a telegraph office to send the news to Craig. That night there was a great bonfire on the main corner of Craig to celebrate our victory.

ELEVEN

Peddling Bulls by the Steak

My twelve years as county and district attorney kept me busy until the Democratic landslide of November 1932 put me out of public office. However, Eunice and I found time in those years to raise a family and to build up our herd of registered Herefords until our Dawson Cattle Company was the largest on Colorado's Western Slope. Our daughter Rosamond—named for our first Elkhead schoolmarm, Rosamond Underwood Perry—was born in 1923. Our second son, Willis, born in 1929, was named for my youngest brother, Willis Vincent Carpenter, who drowned in Illinois at the age of nine.

There was another person named Willis, too, whom the Carpenters admired in the 1920s. William Willis, the brother-in-law of James A. Funkhauser, a president of the American Hereford Association. Before he died, Funkhauser had developed the best milking Herefords in the United States. William Willis became manager of the Funkhauser herd, and it was he who showed me how to acquire heavy Hereford milkers by selecting bulls with well-developed rudimentary teats in front of the scrotum. The theory is disputed, but after we bought two Funkhauser bulls with that development we got so much milk in our mother cows that for years we had to use milking tubes to drain out milk that the calves could not absorb. Later we bought a bull from Funkhauser's widow at Willis's urging, Beau Blanchard 64th, which greatly improved the size and growth of our calves. We enjoyed buying bulls from Mrs. Funkhauser because after the sale she always treated us to a glass of wine and freshly baked angel food cake.

My father died in 1928, leaving my mother as the principal stockholder of the Guthmann, Carpenter and Telling shoe factory in Holland, Michigan. Although I knew nothing about the shoe business, I represented my mother at one of the annual stockholders' meetings. The salesmen were there from all over the country, and I enjoyed talking to them about the business. They asked me why we did not brand our cattle on the neck instead of on the hip, where the best shoe leather could be found. I had no answer except to say that we followed traditions of handling and branding cattle that had been passed down from Mexico in the seventeenth century, and I added that beef buyers paid the same no matter where we branded them. As I talked to them, it crossed my mind that perhaps I should be filling my father's place as head of the factory. But I realized that this was impossible. Ever since my teenage days in New Mexico, I had known that my true calling was the cattle business. These salesmen at the annual meeting were packing new-style shoes into trunks to take as samples to impress retailers and obtain orders for the future. They told me that showing samples to the buyers was the best way to arouse their interest.

In all of this, I noted how aggressively the salesmen pushed their products, and I realized that I had been backward and unimaginative in selling my own. And in that year of 1929, when the stock market crashed and hard times followed, the need to sell was critical. As my own sales dwindled, I tried selling bulls on credit and soon had enough promissory notes to paper our living room. Ninety of our bull calves had been weaned, but it was no use driving them around to sell because nobody had any money. So I decided to try a new way of luring customers to the Dawson Ranch. I hired a movie cameraman from Denver to come to Hayden and make a film of my cattle in action. The high point of the film occurred when we persuaded the whole herd to swim across the Yampa River. Neither the cameraman nor I had had any experience with a project on this scale—swimming a hundred or more spooked cattle across a swiftly flowing river two hundred feet wide in flood. The cameraman and my cowboys all had to learn the hard way.

We found out right away that a big bunch of cattle cannot be crowded into a river. Seeing that it's deep, they just mill around and around. The only way to get the herd to start across the river is to have two cowboys get on each side of a cow and then shove and pull her into the water. When she looks across the river and sees the other side, she will start to swim. The moment she strikes out, the cowboys behind her can urge another cow to follow, and soon the whole herd will get into the water.

During our filmmaking, I learned a few things about swimming horses, too. When a green horse carrying the weight of a rider reaches deep water, where it cannot touch bottom, the horse lunges, and the rider must be cautious. His weight puts the horse under water, and he has to get off the horse or it will drown. So he slides off the horse's rear and grabs its tail, being careful to drop off when they reach shallow water before he gets kicked. I learned that a rider should never pull the bridle to one side of a swimming horse. That tips it over. To guide the horse, he must spatter a little water on the horse's face, which will turn it where he wants it to go.

In the film, getting the calves across was another big problem. To accomplish this, a cowboy would rope a calf by the neck and one of its front legs, dally the rope around the saddle horn, spur the horse into the river as fast as it would go (the rope holding the calf's head above water) and, once across, throw the calf and twist its ear. With this, the calf would bawl, and the frantic mother, hearing her calf's lament, would flop into the river and swim over to the rescue.

It took several hundred feet of film to make the ten-minute movie. I then went to the motion-picture houses in the cow counties and asked them to exhibit it. At first the owners were suspicious of this kind of free advertising. But when I offered to buy enough tickets for each of my cattle-buying customers for a Saturday night, they agreed to show my movie. I explained my plan to them: I would allow my prospective buyers just one free ticket, but when the rancher got it the rest of his family would want to see the show, too, and he would have to buy their tickets at the regular price.

The plan worked quite well. My first show was at Kremmling in Middle Park. The movie house was crammed with ranchers and their families. When the film of my herd swimming the flooded Yampa River began, the excitement of the audience was intense. "Who—ee!" they yelled and whistled when a big cow braved the strong current with her calf on the downstream side.

To my amazement, when the regular feature started, the entire audience stomped and screamed, demanding a rerun of my cattle film, and the owner complied. So my first try at cinema advertising was a great success. I made it a point to pass out my cards in the doorway of a movie house as the audience came out. While doing this I also shook hands with the ranchers and got their promises to come to the Dawson Ranch soon and look over those ninety unsold weaned bull calves. Since the Kremmling showing brought many buyers to our ranch, I took it on the road to Rifle, Meeker, Craig, and Steamboat Springs.

If 1929 was a bad year for selling bulls, 1932 was much worse. We Republicans worried about what that wild Democrat, Franklin D. Roosevelt, would do when he moved into the White House to replace our tried and true Republican president, Herbert Hoover.

I was most unhappy because I had eighty-eight fine registered Hereford bull calves on feed in our corral waiting to be sold, and they were eating us out of house and home. When I wrote an old customer at the Santa Margarita Ranch near San Diego, he answered that he needed my bulls but could not afford the expense of coming to Hayden to see them.

It was my habit to ask myself what my late father would have advised me to do in such a crisis. I could hear him saying, "*Do* something, Ferry. Even if it's the wrong thing, *do* it!" I decided to go on the road like the shoe salesmen—taking a couple of samples to the customers in California. I thought that the Pacific Coast was my best bet because the depression was moving slowly westward from New York. My timing was bad in one way—I would be traveling in the dead of winter in January 1933—but there was my father urging me on: "Even if . . ."

For all the wildness of the project, I was persuaded to try it because my ranch manager, Evan Marr, was willing to go along with me. In his mid-thirties, Evan was a Yankee born in Barre, Vermont—by coincidence my father's hometown. He, too, was a homesteader and a cattle rancher who had worked at the First National Bank in Hayden. He had married a Hayden girl, and as things turned out, he would be my ranch foreman for sixteen years. He was dedicated, prudent, and had the gift of humor, which helped him to be as fine a manager as I ever knew.

It was a cold and gloomy mid-January day with a feeling of snow in the air when Evan and I set out for California. We had selected two average bull calves from our eighty-eight and broke them to halter. We greased up our 1½-ton Model A Ford truck, checked our four-wheel mechanical brakes, and filled the radiator with three gallons of wood alcohol. My son Ed and daughter, Rosamond, watched these preparations with great interest, as did our youngest, Willis, aged four. Next we loaded the truck with feed and bedding. On top of the cab we tied a bedroll holding a quarter of beef from which we would cut steaks to use as barter for gasoline. Finally, we ran the two sample calves up the chute and onto the canvas-covered truck bed.

Eunice and the children and our herdsman, George ("Scotty") Annand, gathered around us to wish us Godspeed on our great adventure. We had photos of the eighty-six other bull calves to show to prospective buyers and a Brownie Kodak for taking pictures along the way, which we would mail back to Eunice. We said goodbye to everyone, pretending to be gay, but Evan and I had sobering thoughts. The bawling of the calves was a soft foreboding, and the little truck, which had rarely gone farther from home than Craig, seventeen miles away, seemed awfully frail for a journey of several thousand miles.

Nevertheless, we headed west on U.S. 40 through Craig, Maybell, and Vernal, Utah. All went well, though we got stuck on Strawberry Pass near Heber City with snowslides all around us. After a two-day delay, county agents in Beaver, Cedar City, and St. George helped us unload and exhibit our calves, but we made no sales. At Mesquite, Nevada, we found that the bridge over the Virgin River had been washed out. Farmers were hauling cars across the river on hayracks. Since our truck was too big for that, we hired a young farmer to unhook his team from his wagon and hitch onto our front bumper to pull us across. He rode on one of the horses, and all went well until we got in the middle of the dirty, brown river, where we hit a spot of soft sand, and the truck sank to the hubs. The team could not move it. Plainly scared, the driver wanted to unhook his team and go back to shore. After some argument, Evan and I got out into the river and heaved and pushed the truck until it headed downstream, where the flow of the river helped us reach the riverbank about fifty yards below our entrance point. I paid the teamster five dollars and we continued on our way. As we left, I asked him how Virgin River got its name. "I don't know for sure," he answered, "but I've been told she's so muddy that no one has ever seen her bottom."

When we got beyond Las Vegas to the California boundary, we had to be inspected for plant diseases before we were allowed to enter the state. We had health papers for the calves but had to unload the feed and bedding before we could continue. This left the truck floor so slippery that the calves could not stand up. When we stopped at a ranch to buy fresh bedding, the owner would not sell us straw until I had unrolled our quarter of beef and asked him how thick he liked his steak. He mellowed after that and sold us two bales of hay and asked us to have dinner with him. He had a strong home-brew which we enjoyed freely—a bit too freely. Driving back to the highway, we missed a turn and ran through an apple orchard. Evan, who was driving, swore that we were lost in England's Sherwood Forest and that Robin Hood would show up any minute.

We got to Hollywood just at dusk and found my father's cousins, the Meads, who had a big colonial house on Hollywood Boulevard. We turned the Model A and our cargo of calves into their elegant driveway without noticing a low-hanging trellis covered with grapevines. Our high sideboards took the whole trellis with us into the Meads' backyard. Luckily, they had been cattle people from North Dakota and did not mind having to re-habilitate their trellis. They also let us unload the weary calves and tie them to an avocado tree. The next day we washed the calves off with a garden hose before leaving for the big Santa Margarita Ranch to show them to Harry Manning. Harry liked them but said that he had just returned from Kansas City, where he had purchased fifty yearling bulls that were all he would need for the year. We asked him to suggest some ranchman who might need a bull calf, and he advised us to see George Sawday, the president of the California Cattlemen's Association, who might be interested.

Sawday lived at Ramona, northeast of San Diego. On our way there it began to rain—not the kind of rain we knew in Routt County but big bucketfuls of water. We had taken off our canvas cover, and the poor little bull calves looked like drowned rats. One of them began coughing and we were afraid they might come down with pneumonia. The Ramona road turned off at Escondido. We planned to stay overnight there and go on to Ramona the next day.

TOP: *Evan Marr (left) and Farrington (right) at the start of their trip to California. Between them, from left to right, are Rosamond, Edward, and Willis.* BOTTOM: *Earl Salisbury stands with Indian children at Taos, New Mexico, while selling bulls by sample, 1943.*

To our surprise, none of the motor courts would rent rooms to trucks with live animals in them. After a couple of these refusals I walked some distance ahead of the truck and rented a room, paid for it, and got the key before the owner saw our truck. I signaled Evan to drive in and park. Just then the calves began to cough and bawl. The proprietor rushed up exclaiming that he was not running a stockyard and would not take our calves in. In turn, I told him that I had paid my bill and would not leave. He agreed to let us stay if we would be gone the next morning at daylight before his regular customers began to awaken.

Early next morning we drove to Ramona, which was high in the hills. The rain had turned to snow and little rivers were running down the gutters of the streets. We found one restaurant open, parked the truck in front, and went inside to get breakfast. The proprietor, who also served as the cook, was in the kitchen playing a violin. I asked him to play "The Arkansas Traveler" so that I could dance a hoedown. Evan sang the words of the chorus, and we had a pleasant interlude for a while until the front door swung open and a tall man appeared in a large black hat with a sheriff's star on his coat.

"Who owns that truck with the cattle in it?" he demanded. I said I did, and he led us outside and showed us that we had parked in such a way that our front wheels had dammed up the water running down the curb. It was overflowing the sidewalk and going into the basement window of an adjacent men's store.

"I'll have to take you in for violating an ordinance," the sheriff said. Of all things, I thought, we make it safely a thousand miles from Hayden only to end up in jail. The "Arkansas Traveler" fiddler, however, proved to be a real friend. He persuaded the sheriff to let us go if we left town at once before the store owner saw the damage that we had done to his basement.

When we finally met George Sawday, he was most helpful. His wife fed us breakfast and Sawday gave us fresh bedding. He suggested that Louis Moulton in the valley might be interested in buying bull calves. As it was still slushy, we kept on our four-buckle galoshes—our "Arctics" as the children called them. When we got to Louis Moulton's ranch we saw a sign announcing "Purebred Hereford Cattle." I rang the doorbell and the woman who answered said that Mr. Moulton was in his office between the house and the barn. We found him there fast asleep on a couch. He looked like the retired city man that he was.

He unhooked the screen door and asked us what our business was. He knew nothing about cattle, he said, but had a well-qualified manager who did all the buying for him. We went into his office, began telling him about our trip from Hayden, and showed him a photo of our truck being towed across the Virgin River.

Moulton paid little attention to our efforts to interest him in bulls and kept staring at our overshoes. "I haven't seen four-buckle overshoes since I left Vermont," he said.

Immediately I saw an opportunity. "My grandfather," I said, "was a practicing physician in Barre, Vermont, and Evan was born there, too. My father was born in East Randolph. My family always considered themselves Green Mountain people."

Suddenly Moulton's face lit up. "How much did you say you wanted for your bulls?" he asked.

"Seventy-five dollars apiece," I said. "No money down, no contract to sign. Your word is good. We'll ship my eighty-six bull calves from Hayden to the Los Angeles stockyard. If your foreman finds that they aren't as good as these two sample bulls here, you needn't take any of them."

"Send me two," Moulton said, "and if the others measure up to your claims, I'll take some more."

That turned the trick for my sample sales program. At each ranch we announced that we were shipping eighty-six bulls, just like the two in the truck, to Los Angeles and asked how many could we send the ranchers. It worked beautifully. In three days we had sold all eighty-eight bull calves as well as the samples.

We drove our empty truck to Whittier and spent the night with "Cousin Nellie" Morse, John Mead's sister. She was a New England housekeeper and everything in her house was immaculate. Since Evan and I had not had a bath the whole trip, that night we took advantage of our private bathroom. While we were at it, we filled the tub with soapy water and washed our underwear, socks, and shirts. Having no iron to press them, we hung the damp clothing over the stained-mahogany door to the bathroom. That left a big white scar on the door, but the Morses forgave us all our boorishness.

The next day—March 6, 1933—the news came over the radio that President Roosevelt had declared a national four-day bank holiday, suspending all transactions. We had picked up a lot of silver dollars in Nevada, where nobody had any use for paper money, and decided to fill our empty Model A with crates of oranges that we planned to sell at a profit when we got to Hayden. At the first roadside orange stand that appeared we priced the crates at $2.75 each. We offered the orange seller a dollar a crate, payable in silver, and advised him that real money would soon be scarce because the president had closed all the banks. He called to his wife, who was listening to the radio, and she confirmed our dire warning. Hurriedly the man filled our truck with crates of oranges at nearly a third of his posted selling price.

During our three-day drive from Los Angeles to Hayden, we had to park the truck in heated garages at night to keep the oranges from freezing. But Evan and I made it home safely without further incident and sold the oranges at $3.00 per crate. That money, in addition to what we got for the steaks that we cut off the beef quarter as needed, covered our traveling expenses for the entire trip. In fact, that peddling trip to California went so well that we tried it again in 1934 with even greater success. The Model A carried us and the calves to Deming, New Mexico, where we made a sale of one hundred calves at one hundred dollars each, along with a contract to deliver that many for five years running. And this contract led to another with a rancher in Mexico by way of Eagle Pass, Texas.

An important result of these five-year contracts was that they assured an outlet for more than half of our bull calves over long periods. It also gave me more time for my law practice and for duties pertaining to the beef industry at large. And such duties soon turned up. Routt County did not escape the anguish of the depression in 1934 that crushed the spirits of Americans everywhere. Still worse for cattlemen, that year was the driest in memory. The Yampa River went dry in spots and the stench of dead fish hung over Hayden. The prices for cattle were at their lowest in forty years, and shipments of cattle to distant markets did not sell for enough to pay for their transportation.

To alleviate the situation, George Watson, president of the Western Slope Cattlemen's Federation, which included all of the Western Slope cattle associations, sent out a call for a mass meeting in Rifle, Colorado. Watson had been foreman of a big cattle outfit for many years and was now semiretired but still serving a term as county commissioner of Eagle County. With other delegates from the Routt-Moffat County Cattle Association,

I attended that meeting at Rifle. It appeared that Edward T. Taylor, a beloved Colorado congressman who represented the Western Slope, was not in sympathy with the New Deal crowd in the White House. Neither was the Colorado governor, "Big Ed" Johnson from Craig. Both were Democrats but they had trouble wielding much influence with the Roosevelt administration. After a day of testimony that included grievances and hardships, the Rifle delegates voted to send a special representative to Washington to present the cattlemen's predicament and have beef designated a basic commodity. I was chosen for that purpose and four hundred dollars was raised to pay for my travel and lodging expenses.

When I got to Washington, I checked in at the Harrington Hotel. The room rates sounded so high to me that I got a cot in the dormitory on the attic floor, where the bellboys slept, for two dollars a night. The next morning I went at once to call on Congressman Taylor, who told me that Washington was full of agricultural lobbyists, all seeking to have their own ailing commodity designated basic so as to be eligible for federal assistance.

Although Ed Taylor was a Democrat and I a Republican, we had been good friends for years. During my call I reminded him of the time in 1928 when I was campaigning on the Republican ticket to be elected district attorney and he was running for Congress on the Democratic ticket. Together we had gone to the Grand County fair in Kremmling to pass out cards and shake hands with the voters. I had admired the way he placated two groups that had each put up a candidate for postmastership in his district. He put his arms around the shoulders of the rival managers and said, "Whenever you boys get together and decide which candidate should get the job, I'll follow your advice and see that the person you want becomes postmaster."

Ed Taylor was an unassuming, down-to-earth, sagacious politician. He had protected the interests of Colorado's Western Slope in Washington since 1909, and his congressional district, encompassing thirty-five counties totaling 61,207 square miles, was one of the largest in the United States. That huge area made his district larger than the size of eastern states such as New York, Pennsylvania, and Ohio. At the same time, he represented a small population of about 100,000 people—only 1.6 people per square mile. Having been elected to Congress sixteen times, he carried great prestige as majority leader and at seventy-seven years was the oldest member of the House of Representatives. Born in Illinois in 1858, Taylor made it through high school in Kansas, became superintendent of schools in Leadville, Colorado, and settled down to the practice of law in Glenwood Springs in 1887. He served as city and county attorney and sat for three terms in the Colorado senate. In short, what Ed Taylor did not know about the Western Slope when he went to Washington in 1909 was not worth knowing. Now, in Congress, he was chairman of the Public Lands Committee, which made him second in power only to the Speaker of the House.

Congressman Taylor told me that the Agriculture Committee of the House was considering an amendment to the Agricultural Adjustment Act which would provide help from the federal treasury for bolstering our cattle markets if Congress designated cattle a basic commodity. He advised me to present my facts to Marvin Jones from Texas, the chairman of the committee on agriculture, and to ask for his help. Failing to find the man in his office, I went up to the door leading to the floor of the House. I asked an elderly guard, a G.A.R. veteran, to send a note to Mr. Jones that I would like to see him. In a short time the congressman came charging out like an angry bull, grabbed me by the arm, and said, "We all know who you are. You're bellyaching for the meat packers. The less I see of you around here, the better I'll like it."

Next I called on Harold M. Stephens, a Salt Lake City lawyer, whom I had met at the Fort Douglas training camp in 1916. He was now a federal circuit court judge and knew his way around Washington. He gave me an introduction to Jerome Frank, solicitor general of the Agriculture Department. Frank told me to draft an amendment to add cattle to the list of basic commodities and send it to the Agriculture Committee. He added that the best person to draft such an amendment was an associate solicitor in the South Building. I found this young man to be slim, fresh-looking, and soft-spoken. He listened intently to what I had to say and asked me to return at 2:00 P.M. When I did, he gave me a typed amendment making cattle a basic commodity and told me to file it with the committee. When I asked his name he replied, "Alger Hiss."

A few days later I was astonished to read in the *Washington Star* that the basic commodity act had been amended—and one paragraph of the amendment was in the exact words that Alger

Hiss had written for me. Elated, I went to Ed Taylor's office and asked him how the amendment had been passed so unexpectedly. He laughed and said, "That's only one of the mysterious things that happen in this city."

TWELVE

The Taylor Grazing Act

When my mission as a lobbyist to amend the basic commodity section of President Roosevelt's Agricultural Adjustment Act succeeded, I went back to Ed Taylor's office to say goodbye. I had exhausted the four hundred dollars that the Western Slope Cattlemen's Federation had given to me, and when I could no longer pay for my bellboy's cot at the Harrington, Taylor let me sleep on a big leather lounge in his outer office. I almost thought of putting a hot plate there to cook my meals. But just then I received a three-hundred-dollar check for rail fare, Pullman berth, and dining car meals on my trip back to Denver. The check was from an old friend from Illinois, Henry B. Babson, a cousin of the economist Roger Babson. Henry, who supported our lobbying, owned a lot of coal lands around Pilot Knob near my Oak Point homestead, and he leased them to cattlemen for grazing.

Ed Taylor asked me if I had read the grazing bill that he had prepared as chairman of the Public Lands Committee. I replied that indeed I had known about the bill, which he had been sponsoring for many years. It proposed to set aside up to eighty million acres of unclaimed public domain in ten western states for grazing purposes. I added that I believed that it would be a fine thing—especially now for the impoverished western livestock industry. With that Ed took me by the arm and marched me into the room where his grazing bill was being discussed by his Public Lands Committee at the urging of President Roosevelt's new secretary of the interior, Harold L. Ickes.

The members of the committee asked me what I knew about public lands. I answered that I had lived next to the public domain in northwestern Colorado since 1905. I said that I had also worked next to the big cow outfits of Routt and Moffat counties until both the influx of homesteaders and the cattlemens' own overgrazing of the open range had put many of them out of business. I had taken up a homestead of my own in 1907, I said, and was still running cattle on it as well as on the adjoining free open range.

When the meeting was opened for questions some members said that the remaining public lands should be turned over to the states in which they were situated. They argued that the various state land boards which now had control of the school lands— granted to the states by the federal government at the time of their admission to the Union—could regulate grazing on the public domain better than the federal government. I replied that the state governments had no experience in the regulation of grazing. Furthermore, because of the large interstate movements of sheep, it would be difficult for the states to attempt it. I then pushed hard for federal control. Only a federal agency, I argued, could do a good job of preserving the pasturage value of the public lands.

Back in Hayden, I forgot all about Ed Taylor's grazing bill and its support by Secretary Ickes. I attended the annual meeting of the American National Cattlemen's Association in Albuquerque and defended the New Deal's Agricultural Adjustment Act. As I was a lifelong Republican, some of my friends thought I had gone haywire. I also went to the Wyoming stockgrower's convention in Cheyenne and applauded the talk of the secretary of agriculture, Henry A. Wallace, the hybrid-corn expert, who advocated governmental aid and supervision of agriculture. These ideas were anathema to western cattlemen.

In Wyoming I also debated with my old friend and fellow Princetonian, Dan Casement, who was perhaps the most colorful of western cattlemen. Dan was a son of General Jack Casement, who had built the Union Pacific Railroad across Wyoming. He stated that raising cattle was not a business but a way of life. I felt that way, too, I replied, but as a practical matter, cattle raising was entitled to legislative protection like any other business. Shortly after this debate, Chester Davis, administrator of the Agricultural Adjustment Act, asked me to serve cattle interests in an advisory way for the Department of Agriculture. When the adjustment act was declared unconstitutional, Chester Davis proposed a soil conservation bill to replace it. Congress passed the bill and it was approved by the Supreme Court.

Early in July 1934 I learned that the Taylor Grazing Act had been passed by Congress and signed by President Roosevelt on June 28. I took a few days off at home in Hayden to study the bill in relation to my own use of the public domain and to the history of American agriculture in general. The Taylor Grazing Act pertained to that immense part of the public domain—an area larger than the entire states of Texas and California combined—which remained unclaimed by any person, state, railroad, Indian tribe, national park, national forest, or other agency of the federal government. It encompassed most of the intermountain region between the Rockies on the east and the Sierra and Cascades on the west. With less than half the annual rainfall of the Middle West, its agricultural use was sharply limited. Crop raising was restricted to irrigated lands near streams—as along the Yampa River and its branches in Routt County. Sixty-four percent of this unclaimed land was fit only for livestock grazing.

I read in the preamble to the Taylor Grazing Act that its purpose was "to stop injury to the public grazing lands by preventing overgrazing and soil deterioration, to provide for their orderly use, improvement and development, to stabilize the livestock industry dependent upon the public range, and for other purposes." It also gave the Department of the Interior broad powers to bring this neglected land empire out of its isolation and into the mainstream of the nation's economic life. The Department of the Interior was authorized by the act to develop water power, control soil erosion, and issue grazing permits to qualified raisers of cattle and sheep. A key and unique feature was the classification of this unclaimed public domain in ways that would allow it to be used to best advantage. To administer the act, the secretary of the interior would appoint the director of a Division of Grazing to organize the public domain into grazing districts.

As I continued my study of the terms of this legislation, I felt that it constituted one of the most important advances in the entire history of the public domain. It was the first attempt by Congress to add "grass" to the list of those natural resources that

RIGHT: *Farrington R. Carpenter (left) and Congressman Edward T. Taylor, 1935.* BOTTOM: *First Grazing Service Conference, September 3, 1935, Salt Lake City, Utah. From left to right are (front row): G. G. Frazer, Milo H. ("Mike") Demming, Marvin Klemme, Joe H. Leach, A. H. Shank, and E. H. Franzell. Second row: L. R. Brooks, J. Q. Peterson, Warren Sholes, R. E. Morgan, Depue Falck, and Guy T. Williams. Third row: G. M. ("Jerry") Kerr, A. D. ("Bud") Molohan, Archie D. Ryan, Charles F. ("Frank") Moore, Farrington R. Carpenter, and E. D. ("Tiny") Greenslet. Other delegates not pictured were John F. Deeds, Ed J. Keefe, C. F. ("Bud") Dierking, and Milton Fairmaux.*

should be conserved and whose productivity should be improved. At the outset, the act segregated a maximum of eighty million acres of grasslands in ten western states where public lands greatly exceeded privately owned acres. The ten states were Colorado, Wyoming, New Mexico, Idaho, Utah, Nevada, Montana, Oregon, Arizona, and California.

To explain the new grazing law to the people of those ten states, a party of officials under the leadership of a Coloradan whom I knew well, Oscar L. Chapman, was sent out to hold public meetings. Chapman was assistant secretary of the Department of the Interior, and with him was Thomas Havell, who represented the venerable General Land Office (GLO). Created in 1812 to distribute the public domain, the GLO by 1934 had very little public land left to distribute.

In these meetings, whenever questions arose about the meaning of words or phrases in the Taylor Grazing Act, Havell would settle the issue by saying crisply, "That's a matter entirely within the discretion of Mr. Ickes, the secretary of the interior." This answer gave westerners the impression that the range livestock business was going to be under the limited control of a distant bureaucrat in Washington who, in the words of one cowboy, "didn't know which end of a cow got up first."

When Oscar Chapman reached Salt Lake City, he asked me to meet him there, and I did. He explained that Secretary Ickes had read my testimony before the Public Lands Committee. The secretary was looking for a director of the new grazing division, and he wanted me to come to Washington for an interview. Chapman had suggested my name because I had served as attorney for cattlemen's associations and had had enough business with the sheep crowd to be familiar with their grazing problems.

In Washington I went at once to Ed Taylor's office and reread the draft of the grazing act. I noted particularly its authorization for the secretary of the interior "to cooperate with local associations of stockmen" to carry out its purposes. Here, I thought, was an opportunity for local stockmen to help guide a federal grazing program in a practical way and not have all the important decisions made in Washington—as was the case with grazing in the national forests. It looked like a chance to bring in much-needed democratic processes in place of the old bureaucratic methods of absentee control of public lands. The act seemed to authorize the secretary of the interior to coordinate range management and to cooperate with local groups of stockmen in ways never tried before.

Ed Taylor and Oscar Chapman set up my interview with Secretary Ickes, about whom Ed had given me some biographical data. "Harold L. Ickes," he warned me, "makes a virtue of being crusty and irascible. He doesn't have much sense of humor, and he enjoys calling himself, 'the old curmudgeon.' " Ed concluded, "One more thing. Watch your step with Ickes. He's ambitious and crafty. He is an S.O.B. in some ways, and he's no ordinary politician."

I found the curmudgeon enthroned behind a huge desk at the far end of a long, narrow office. As I entered, I imagined him watching me as warily as a tiger watches a visitor at the zoo. He was sixty years old, bespectacled, stocky, and smoked a cigarette held in a quill-like holder. I knew that he had grown up around Chicago and had graduated cum laude from the University of Chicago Law School in 1907. Then he had gone into Cook County politics as a Bull Mooser and progressive Republican but had become a Democrat after President Harding's election. Later he attracted the attention of Franklin D. Roosevelt as an expert on civil liberties and conservation. Roosevelt found him to be a valuable asset in his presidential campaign because of his energy in rounding up voters and his furious diatribes against big business.

Secretary Ickes began the interview by asking me if there were any reasons why I could not serve as director of the Grazing Division. I told him I could think of three. First, I was a Republican and did not intend to change my political affiliation. To that, the secretary said, "As far as your politics go, I don't care what they are if you keep your mouth shut and don't go around saying things against the New Deal." I said that I could do that. Second, I added, I did not want to be responsible for creating a great centralized bureau like the National Forest Service, run from Washington by eastern people who knew little about the public domain. Ickes replied that he planned a small bureau and had estimated $150,000 for the first year's cost of the Grazing Division. He expected to have the administration of the act decentralized from Washington. Third, I said, I had played a prominent part in the cattle-sheep wars of northwestern Colorado in the 1920s and my appointment would be distasteful to the wool growers. He replied that he would investigate the matter.

The next day, Oscar Chapman told me that Secretary Ickes had talked on the phone with Wilson McCarthy, a sheep owner who was the attorney for the National Woolgrowers' Association. McCarthy and I had been on opposite sides of several cattle-sheep lawsuits. When Ickes asked him whether he thought that I could be fair in dealing with the two rival livestock interests, McCarthy had answered "Yes." Thus Ickes recommended me to the president as director of the Division of Grazing of the Taylor Grazing Act. I was duly appointed and accepted the position.

A few days later, Secretary Ickes called me back, thanked me for taking the job, and said, "There's no money here to pay you. You can draw $6,500 a year, which I'll have to take out of my personal appropriation. We'll detach fifteen or sixteen men from the U.S. Geological Survey who have classified land in the West and know the country. They are all college graduates and you can use them to set this act up." That was about all in the way of instruction that the secretary told me.

I left the room with his first assistant secretary, Ebert K. Burlew, who described to me the far-flung activities of the Department of the Interior. I was impressed by Burlew's efficiency and loyalty to "Mr. Secretary," and I could see that he was the day-by-day boss of the Interior Department.

"Now you will have to travel around a bit," Burlew said, and he gave me a little book with green sheets in it. All I had to do was to go to a railroad station and sign one of those slips for a ticket, a Pullman, and my meals. The little green book made me feel that I was on my way. But I had misgivings. I had never sought to be even a *little* bureaucrat in a small mountain town like Hayden, and here I was not only a bureaucrat but one with a capital B!

Feeling that I ought to be doing something important, I went around to the GLO to find out where those millions of grazing acres were. I told the clerk that I needed a map of the remaining public domain.

"Map?" the clerk said. "Why, there isn't such a map."

"Well," I said, "you've been in business long before there was a Department of the Interior. Didn't you ever map your lands?"

The clerk said that the GLO had nineteen land offices scattered over the West that received entries daily for public lands. The township plats showing these changes were kept in the local offices. He explained that the only way that I could locate the grazing lands was to map out my grazing districts from these township plats.

A certain gleam in his eye made me understand what I was up against. The GLO had lived on public land filings for a century, and it would take me years to visit all those land offices to examine their township plats. If I did the mapping instead of leaving it to all those GLO people it would put them out of work. So here was my first run-in with my old bugaboo—bureaucracy.

I soon saw that I was involved also in a tug-of-war between federal agencies. Secretary Ickes wanted to enlarge the Department of the Interior and to rename it the Conservation Department. He was also maneuvering to have the National Forest Service transferred from the Department of Agriculture back to Interior, which had lost it during Theodore Roosevelt's reform days, when both Interior and the GLO were accused of fraud, bribery, and large-scale theft of public lands.

Secretary Ickes, I learned, was pleased with the Taylor Grazing Act because it gave him control not only of the specified 80 million acres but of the entire unclaimed public domain totaling more than 140 million acres. This control and the hundreds of extra employees needed to classify it and to manage the grazing districts would make the Department of the Interior the largest land agency of the United States government. To ensure Interior's control of my Division of Grazing, Ickes put his Division of Investigations—a sort of private eye—and the GLO in charge of handling land transfers as part of the administration of the grazing act.

The men that the secretary had assigned to me from the United States Geological Survey to classify grazing districts had no knowledge of livestock, but they were skilled mapmakers—and they knew where the nation's water was. I had learned from my little spring at Oak Point that water would be a guiding principle when I got to the matter of assigning grazing permits. The permits would be useless to ranchers unless they had water on their property to keep livestock alive during those seasonal times when none was available on the arid grasslands.

Since, as the Wyoming cowboy had said, nobody in Washington seemed to know which end of a cow gets up first, I was encouraged when Rexford Tugwell, assistant secretary of the Department of Agriculture, agreed to loan me a man I had always admired, Edward M. Kavanaugh, the best of the Forest Service grazing supervisors in ten states. Tugwell also arranged to loan me Ernest Winkler, chief of wildlife and range management. Dismissing my fear that it was not politic to seek aid outside of the Department of the Interior, he said that organizing grazing districts merited the help of whatever government agency. But I suspected that my visit with Tugwell at Agriculture did not sit well with Secretary Ickes, who kept alive the old feud between Interior and Agriculture. He was eager to remove the cloud that had shadowed Interior ever since the Teapot Dome scandals.

Because my job as director of the Grazing Division was peripatetic, I was not required to live in Washington. However, Eunice came to the nation's capital that summer to look at my plush office with its mahogany desk full of call buttons and aides running about looking at me respectfully. We stayed at the Harrington Hotel—but this time in style, not in the bellboys' attic. Meanwhile, Eunice moved around town to find an apartment for the winter months, during which Evan Marr would be in charge of the home place in our absence.

When a few days of free time came along, Eunice asked me to take her to Boston, which she had never seen, to visit my law school campus at Harvard. So we took the Federal Express from Washington over a weekend. I had developed a habit through the years of concealing my eastern background and stressing my western identity by wearing bright-colored shirts, a cowman's carved leather belt, cowboy boots, and a rancher's broad-brimmed hat. At the same time, however, I was both proud and aware of my Vermont Yankee heritage.

When we arrived in Boston we first went to Boston Commons. There, on a plaque, I read that we were standing on the corner of twenty-five acres that the colonists had used for training militia—in addition to grazing their livestock. I wondered how they had regulated their grazing land three hundred years and more ago. Then we went to the Boston Public Library, where we ended up in the reference room on its second floor. Approaching a gray-haired librarian, I said, "I'd like a copy of the grazing regulations on the Boston Commons in 1642, if you please." Without blinking an eye over what must have been an unusual request, she disappeared into a back room and after a while returned with an old leather-bound book, *Grazing Regulations on the Boston Commons.*

I opened the book, saw what I was looking for, and sat down to copy the centuries-old regulations. One provided that there should be a charge of two shillings a week on a horse or a cow, but that a sheep should be charged one fifth of that amount. In the book sheep were described as "lesser cattle," and the ratio at the time was five sheep to one cow. Ministers of the church were allowed to graze their buggy horses without charge, which the regulations termed a "free use permit." Suddenly the thought struck me that this was what we were planning to issue in the West in 1934—free use permits for grazing. I also found that many details of early grazing were similar to what we were using in modern times.

Back in Washington, I made my appearance before the House committee that was reviewing the Department of the Interior's budget for the Taylor Grazing Act. Some Republicans on the committee were trying to nail Interior to the wall on overspending. One congressman, who led off the questioning, was a very bright fellow but sharp-nosed. He had a row of pinpoint-sharpened pencils on the table and a pad right in front of him. Anybody could see, while I was being sworn in, that he could barely wait for me. I was presented to the committee, and I told its members what I was doing and why. Sharp-Nose began to cross-examine me.

"I see you charge five times as much for a cow as you do for a sheep. Why is that?"

"Grazing experts in the Forest Service have determined that one cow can live on what five sheep eat," I answered. After reading off more official figures, I picked up my notes from the Boston Commons grazing records. "And there is nothing new in these figures, Mr. Congressman," I said. "I have here a copy of the records in the Boston Public Library, which I visited yesterday, showing that cattle and sheep consumed forage at that same ratio back in 1642 on the Boston Commons. It hasn't changed in three hundred years." The congressman cleared his throat noisily and signaled to me to go on. I noted that he was perturbed because he had broken the point of the pencil he waved at me.

I went on to the subject of what we called "free-use permits." I explained that in Routt County we allowed homesteaders who owned only a couple of milk cows and a team of horses free use of the grazing lands around them. We followed a precedent that the Forest Service had inaugurated. I checked my notes and referred again to Colonial practices. "On Boston Commons in 1642 the only free-use permit was for the preacher's horse. But that free-use permit for grazing on Boston Commons sets a precedent for our grazing regulations today."

As I was nearing the end of my recital, the door opened and in walked our Colorado congressman, Ed Taylor. He came over to where I was seated in the witness chair at the end of the table and placed his hands on my shoulders. He addressed the committee: "Gentlemen, excuse me for interrupting, but I have something that needs to be said. This young man comes from my district in Colorado. While he's a Republican, he and I are good friends. He's administering this law, the Taylor Grazing Act, which has been named after me. I want to say this. Anything that he asks from you I want you to give him, because he knows what he's doing and he won't ask you for anything that he doesn't need. Thank you."

With that Ed turned and walked out the door. The rest of the congressmen sat with their mouths open. Then the chairman smiled and said, "Mr. Carpenter, you're excused. Just write down what you want. We may as well give it to you because Congressman Taylor will put it in the appropriation bill if we don't."

During an adjournment the next witness, Dr. Mendenall, who was chairman of the U.S. Geological Survey, followed me out into the hall.

"Damn you, Carpenter," he said, "this is the first time you've ever appeared to testify before this hard-boiled committee. And what happened? The chairman of the General Appropriation Committee comes in and tells them to give you anything you want. You get away with the whole works while the rest of us have to spend days justifying every little item." Then, with a grin, he said, "It's too bad I can't find a geological survey record that's three hundred years old."

By mid-August 1934 I was through with appearances before congressional committees. Oscar Chapman phoned to say that I was to conduct the first public meeting to explain the purposes of the grazing act. It would take place at Grand Junction, Colorado, on September 27. Ads were being placed in all western newspapers asking interested cattle and sheep raisers to attend.

Chapman gave me no pointers about conducting the meeting, and I did not ask Secretary Ickes for instructions.

I spent a day or two wandering alone in Washington's Rock Creek Park trying to decide what program I should present to implement the act. I felt rather at a loss—somewhat as I had felt when Jack White and I had smashed up our Indian sales goods returning from Taos long ago.

Since no appropriation to finance the act had been made as yet, I had no money to pay people to organize those 80 million acres of public domain into grazing districts. (Later FDR would enlarge the original 80 million acres under the act to 142 million.) I knew about the Forest Service's stockmen's advisory boards for grazing, but those advisers were never asked to decide anything more important than the best place to put salt on the range or the best day for branding. Important matters were decided by the bureaucrats in Washington.

It seemed to me that these considerations conspired to leave only one way to recruit an agency big enough to bring together intelligently and immediately the wisdom needed to write rules and regulations for the grazing districts. Only range cattlemen and sheepmen could perform that task. They had competed among themselves all their lives for use of the public lands and they knew every acre of it. In addition, they knew the critical importance of water to the livestock industry. If I could create district advisory boards composed of local stockmen, their recommendations would set the tone for the administration of the Taylor Grazing Act. The prestige of these boards, elected by the range users themselves, would attract the most knowledgeable and progressive stockmen.

I returned home to Hayden. As the fateful day of September 27 approached, I was by no means precisely sure how I would conduct the Grand Junction meeting. I shined up my new Ford—not the old Model A truck of our California adventure, but a sporty V-8 convertible with crank-up windows and wire wheels—and once again Eunice and the children waved me goodbye as I set off on U.S. 40 for Grand Junction.

THIRTEEN

The Maverick and the Curmudgeon

Grand Junction, the site of the first meeting of my infant Grazing Division on September 27, 1934, is the largest town on Colorado's Western Slope. It lies at the junction of the Gunnison River and the Grand River (renamed the Colorado River in 1921). The picturesque Book Cliffs guard it on the north, rising above the peach orchards of the fertile river valley. Like most Western Slope towns it is twenty years younger than Denver and the Front Range cities. Settlement did not come until the Ute Indians were removed to Utah from their Western Slope reservation in 1881.

I arrived at Grand Junction to find it full of cattle and sheep raisers from Colorado, Utah, New Mexico, and Wyoming. All of them wanted to know how the Taylor Grazing Act would affect their business. The cattlemen had set up headquarters at La Court Hotel, and the woolgrowers had chosen La Harp Hotel for theirs. Both groups were huddling with their lawyers and watching each other sullenly. The space between the two hotels had the feel of a place awaiting a peace treaty.

So many people gathered around me before I was ready to answer questions that I took a walk out of town. On its outskirts I found a camp with a chuck wagon and a bunch of cowboys getting ready for chow. One of them had been with me in the cattle-sheep wars of the 1920s. Inviting me to join the cowboys for supper, he said, "Ferry, we're busted and can't afford a hotel, so we're camping here with our roundup outfit."

Since Grand Junction had no auditorium big enough for the meeting, we moved to the fairground and took over the exhibition hall. I was happy to discover that Ed Taylor had come over from Glenwood Springs to watch the proceedings. For him the event was the culmination of fifteen-years work trying to get Congress to stop the deterioration of 142 million acres of unclaimed public domain. I needed an old friend like Ed by my side.

When they met in the exhibition hall, the cattlemen sat on one side of the aisle and the sheepmen on the other. They were a grim-looking crowd. I read a letter from Secretary Ickes telling how the Taylor Grazing Act would conserve the public grasslands of the country, which some of them had mistreated by overgrazing. The letter brought the faintest patter of applause. I knew from their expressions that they were remembering Ickes's first act as secretary of the interior, which had been to send in United States marshals to order all their fences on the open range removed.

Congressman Taylor rose to speak and received an ovation. The audience knew that he had devoted his life to protecting the rights of the stockmen to use the open range to their best advantage. He traced the history of the Taylor Grazing Act and introduced me as his friend and a stockman they could trust to treat them fairly.

I spoke next and told the assembly that my job was to find a way to establish on the public domain of ten western states grazing districts based not on directives from bureaucrats in Washington but on the stockmen's personal knowledge of the livestock business. I added that my concern at this first meeting was to set up five grazing districts for Colorado. Although no maps of the public domain were available, I said, the Colorado stockmen in the audience had been competing for Colorado grasslands for decades and knew the location of every unclaimed acre of public domain and its potential for grazing.

I asked the Colorado sheep and cattle groups to caucus separately during the noon hour and went on to suggest that each of the two groups elect an advisory committee of five men. Then I hung a big map of Colorado on the wall and left some crayons before adjourning the meeting until 2:00 P.M. To give them an idea of how the two advisory committees should decide on the five grazing districts for Colorado, I said, "I ask you to mark on the map the natural range districts as you know them. If there is a deep river here, then that would be a district boundary. A high cliff would be another boundary, and so on."

When the stockmen returned after lunch, their two advisory committees had reached agreement on the boundary lines for five Colorado grazing districts and had marked them on the map. Their agreement showed me that cattlemen and sheepmen could work together if they clearly understood the purpose of the grazing act. I pointed out that I had no funds to pay them for serving on the district advisory boards, but when I called for a vote on the advisory board method of managing the grazing districts, the result was 414 in favor to 58 against.

The next problem was an interpretation of the word *near*. According to the act, preferential grazing permits went to those who owned property with water resources "near" the public grazing lands. This put the sheepmen at a disadvantage since their ranches were often long distances from their grazing lands. While the cattlemen argued that "near" meant "adjoining," the sheepmen said that use—not distance—determined their grazing rights.

To settle this complicated "how far is near" issue, I set up a "jury" next day in the federal courtroom. Sitting on the "jury" was one member of the Bureau of Reclamation, three from Soil Conservation, three from the Geological Survey, and two from the Forest Service. During the day lawyers for the cattlemen and the sheepmen argued the question without coming to a decision. Finally, my Forest Service consultant, Ernest Winkler, asked me, "How long have you been in the government service, Mr. Carpenter?"

"Nearly two weeks," I said.

"Do you *have* to decide this 'how far is near' matter today?" he asked.

"No."

"Well," Winkler said, "just let it go, let it go. Never meet a controversial issue like that if you want to hold your government job. Just go along like it isn't there and let the rest of them cry about it."

It seemed like the only sensible solution, so I told the stockmen that we would take the issue under advisement. That, of course, means that you don't know what to do and don't know whether you will ever know what to do. As to the permit issue, I decided to learn what the sentiment was in the other western states before trying to make arbitrary rules.

As I adjourned that first Grand Junction meeting, I was pleased with the progress I had made in setting up local advisory committees for Colorado to administer the grazing act by a system of dual control—sheepmen and cattlemen. It gave me confidence that the same approach would work in the other nine western states. A principle had been established—that each livestock owner was to have one vote in advisory board elections regardless of the number of livestock he owned. This would ensure that no small clique could control the advisory board.

During the five months of meetings that followed, I traveled all over the West, mostly by train and bus but sometimes in my Ford convertible. Throughout those wearisome weeks of travel, I was inspired by the grandeur and immensity of the West, its beauty, and its variety of scene—a variety that I also found in the points of view expressed in the different communities where I held meetings.

In Salt Lake City, the Utah sheepmen and cattlemen gathered in the Hotel Utah on Temple Square. Here, I discovered, everyone in the audience was an orator (the Mormon elders teach their flock to be good public speakers). So many people took this chance to show their training that I commented to a Mormon who sat with me on the platform, "We'll never reach an agreement here. Too many orators."

"Just wait," he said. "The bishop will arrive soon, and when he speaks they'll do what he tells them to do."

And that is exactly what happened. The bishop stood up and wasted no time informing the group of a proper course of action. Another Mormon noted that because the bishop was the top man in his community, people had confidence in his judgment. Furthermore, the State had so few natural resources that the people had to work together to survive. Setting up grazing districts and a committee of advisers was easy in Utah.

However I found a different situation in Boise, Idaho, where the Idaho Wool Growers Association dominated the livestock business. "This Taylor Grazing Act is just what we need," said one of their sheepmen. "We *want* this public domain, all of it, but for sheep—not cattle." While I was battling with those "woolies" they sent a committee to me saying, "We advise you to get out of Idaho and let us settle this matter in our own way, the sheepman's way." Seeing that I could do nothing with them, I left Idaho like a steer heading for the cedars. Later, when the other states learned that Idaho planned to try to run its grazing districts for sheep only, they piled their sheep into Idaho and the Idaho sheepmen asked me to come back and set up grazing districts to keep out "foreign" sheep.

In Arizona and New Mexico I found that the states owned most of the grazing lands and controlled the open range. In Wyoming people believed that the public domain belonged to the state, not to the nation. Initially they claimed that the grazing act was illegal but gradually overcame their hostility and went along with my program. In time they began to realize that the whole point of the Taylor Grazing Act was to increase the livestock potential of their eroded and overgrazed grasslands—a problem that had been neglected for years.

The three states that were the most reasonable in my effort to implement the act were California, Colorado, and Oregon. The last-mentioned state cooperated because Ed Kavanaugh, the Forest Service grazing chief in Oregon, knew his people and saw to it that the State Agricultural College at Corvallis sent its faculty members to my meetings and supplied professional knowledge in the formation of my Oregon advisory boards.

My promotional meetings culminated on February 12, 1935, when Secretary Ickes spent a day in Denver to confer with the multitude of federal and state agencies and railroad landowners who were involved with the operation of the act. I was glad to have the secretary in Denver; his support of the act would help me deal with the opposition I had met in some states over the advisory board plan. I accompanied the secretary on a whirlwind visit that included breakfast at the Brown Palace Hotel with Governor Ed Johnson and a speech to the Colorado legislature.

Previously the secretary had asked me to write parts of a grazing act paper that he delivered to a packed house of stockmen at the Broadway Theater. The section that I wrote praised the livestock owners who had given their time and services free to set up grazing districts, and I put in my hope that the advisory boards would become a permanent part of the Department of the Interior. The stockmen, of course, applauded when the secretary read that line in the paper, thinking it meant legal control of the grazing districts by the local advisory boards. In closing, the secretary described the act as "one step toward the salvation of an inland empire being wasted by neglect." To this he added: "The free and unrestricted use of the public range must give way to a policy of prudent use for the general welfare."

Throughout the summer and into the fall of 1935, I worked on the problems of my stockmen's advisory boards, following the secretary's "policy of prudent use." In the meantime, I had heard no word of dissent from him. Thus I was surprised when, as I wound up a stockmen's meeting in Phoenix, a telegram arrived from the secretary ordering me to return at once to Washington. I took the Santa Fe train that night and hurried into Secretary Ickes's long office, where I was met not only by the secretary but members of his staff arranged in a semicircle around his big desk. These included his assistant secretaries, his solicitor, the commissioner of the GLO, and all the other bureau chiefs. The secretary didn't beat around the bush. Waving his long cigarette holder, he began: "Now I hear what you are doing, Mr. Carpenter, with those advisory committees, and I don't like it. You're not handling your Grazing Division in a way that I approve of at all. I figure that you're selling out to the big operators."

"How do you figure that, Mr. Secretary?" I asked.

Ickes ignored the question. "And you have made some very scurrilous remarks about the Washington government."

"What remark was that, Mr. Secretary?"

"Well," Ickes said, "in Reno you referred to Washington as 'that big county seat on the Potomac.' "

I admitted that I could have said that.

The secretary continued. "Before I fire you, I have a letter here that tells you all the things you've done wrong." He handed me a twelve-page letter. I took it, backed out of the meeting, and read it in the corridor. The letter was so ridiculous that I left Interior and went straight to see what Ed Taylor thought of it. Ed told me that he had gotten through on the phone that same day to President Roosevelt, whom he had known in Washington since 1913. Ed said that the conversation went: "Look here, Mr. President, you can't let Harold Ickes fire the boy I picked for my Taylor Grazing Act job. There is nobody out West as well qualified to handle it." A few days later, word of my reinstatement reached me from the Interior Department.

Nobody likes to be fired, even briefly, from a challenging and interesting job. My interest in the successful feeding of cattle on the range was a deep-seated one, dating from my teens in New Mexico and continuing through all the years of building up a large herd of purebred Herefords in Colorado. Along the way, I had come to know something about grazing cattle and about stockmen. For his part, Harold Ickes had great skill as a politician, but every line of his long letter of complaint revealed that he had no understanding of what was involved in transforming those 142 million acres of unclassified and untended public domain into an active part of the nation's agricultural economy.

The secretary's letter had begun:

> I realize the obstacles in organizing any new service, but it has been my thought from the beginning that with the three established agencies in the Department of the Interior that are principally involved in grazing matters [two of which were the GLO and the Division of Investigations] you should have utilized to a greater extent the services they are capable of rendering without departure from their regular functions. You have never accepted this principle of organization, with the result that you have practically ignored the staffs that were available to you, except the Geological Survey, and, furthermore, instead of setting up an adequate organization of your own you have relied upon a skeleton staff, plus the local advisory committees, for such administrative work as has been accomplished. . . . One of the noteworthy characteristics of the grazing policy under your supervision has been a susceptibility to change, which has been an obstacle to accomplishment. These changes have frequently been made without consulting other responsible officials in the department, including myself, and ill-considered announcements have been made by you personally in public meetings.

The secretary's letter contained a dozen other charges of maladministration by his director of grazing. But it made crystal clear the main point of difference between us. This came down to the role that local stockmen were to play in the implementation of the grazing act. I wanted them to have a significant part in electing their own advisory boards, with the right to discuss and recommend rules and regulations *before* they were promulgated by the Department of the Interior in Washington. The secretary did not favor electing stockmen as advisers—or, as he referred to them, "those pirates." Rather, he wanted to control them through the process of appointment so that they would be subject to his dismissal. He took care to remind me, in particular, that "these local committees are nothing more than advisory bodies. They are not organized or equipped to handle administrative matters nor does the law authorize the Secretary of the Interior to delegate authority to them. You have encouraged these local committees to perform functions—delegating to the committees the entire administration of the Taylor Grazing Act."

This comment forced me to infer that the secretary was afraid that the stockmen's committees intended to usurp his power. In a detailed letter of rebuttal to his charges, which I prepared with my field men, I explained that the last thing my advisory boards wanted was to encroach on his authority. They simply laid out the facts, based on their experience with the livestock industry, that the department could rely on to make sound decisions.

I was inclined to forgive and forget that October firing by the curmudgeon, for I knew that he was not in a tranquil mood that day. With his habit of trying to control everything and everybody, he had taken on too much bureaucratic responsibility even for his vast energy. He was running the Indian Reorganization Act, and he had accepted direction of the Public Works Administration, including the Civilian Conservation Corps. In addition, he was maneuvering to add a bureau or two for Interior from the Department of Commerce and conniving to divorce the National Forest Service from the Department of Agriculture. In the meantime, the Washington press corps was taking pot shots at him daily. The reporters called the Interior Department "the Department of Things in General." And General Hugh Johnson, former head of the National Recovery Administration, labeled Ickes at a press conference as a "triple threat termite." (The curmudgeon countered Johnson's insult by stating that "Old Iron Pants . . . suffers from mental saddle sores.")

Secretary Ickes himself was new in political office. However, he had on his staff two professionals in the art of making employees they disliked anxious to leave of their own accord. One of them was Burlew, the first assistant secretary, and the other was Louis R. Glavis, head of the special agents who served the secretary as unofficial gumshoes. Soon after my reinstatement by President Roosevelt I foolishly mentioned to a *Rocky Mountain News* reporter in Denver—though off the record—that the president would announce the next day that he was withdrawing all the public domain from homestead entry except in Alaska. As I was leaving for a Grazing Division meeting in Utah, the secretary sent an aide who caught me in Union Station with an order to cancel the Utah trip and return to Washington to explain my remark, which had been overheard. In Washington the secretary gave me the worst verbal horsewhipping I had ever had—as though I had leaked a secret about a wartime offensive.

Months before my firing, I had suspected that the secretary was watching me. Hayden friends had told me that Interior employees from Washington had been in town asking questions about my private behavior. Later, Burlew and Glavis passed on to the secretary, as grounds for suspicion of impropriety, the fact that at a meeting in St. George, Utah, I had introduced one of my Mormon committeemen, Wallie Mathis, as "old Slick Ears"—meaning in cow language that he was ever ready to put his brand on any unbranded animal loose on the range. In rebuttal, Wallie told the big crowd of stockmen: "Ferry thinks he has something on me. But I have a good one on him. Last summer he was here at Covered Wagon Days when the girls were competing in foot races. Ferry knew all about those girls and their athletic abilities. He picked the best runner every time. You know why? Ferry had been chasing them girls before." For years thereafter, stockmen on the street in Salt Lake City would yell at me, "Hey, Carpenter, you still chasing them Mormon girls?"

I noticed in these years that Secretary Ickes seemed to take particular pleasure in humiliating members of his staff at biweekly meetings, knowing that they would not defend themselves because of his power to dismiss them from office. Perhaps it irked him that he could not come down on me in the same way because I was a presidential appointee and could not be removed at will. Ernest Gruening, then in charge of Insular Affairs and editor of the *New Republic*, was similarly protected. Once when the secretary failed to appear at a staff meeting, Burlew dismissed us after we had waited for an hour, saying that the secretary was indisposed. Whispering in my ear, Gruening said, "I hope it's nothing trivial."

My reinstatement by the president must have made an impression on Secretary Ickes. Though my feeling was that he continued to be critical of my work, he said nothing directly to me about it. In fact, he was entirely cooperative in July of 1936, when he invited the two chairmen of the cattle and sheep sections of all fifty-four district advisory boards to Washington for a conference. I notified members of Congress from those areas of this meeting so that they could learn how the grazing districts were managed.

When the advisers reached Washington, they wanted to meet President Roosevelt in the White House. A meeting was arranged, and the advisers were ushered into the Oval Office. President Roosevelt was at his best. He greeted all of them with his broad smile and told them that he, too, was a farmer in a small way at Hyde Park. He thanked them for taking time off from their farming duties to help the government make a success of the grazing program. Turning to Secretary Ickes, he said, "Harold, I want to shake the hand of every one of these loyal citizens." Since the secretary knew none of their names, he called me forward to present them to the president, who took each extended hand in both of his and gave it a hearty shake. When we left the White House, Mr. Jamison, an adviser from Arizona, turned to me and said, "I've been a Republican all my life, but no one could ever vote against that man if he ever met him face to face."

It was soon after this meeting that the secretary told me for the first time what he thought the main function of my local advisers ought to be. Several newspapers during that week had mentioned Secretary Ickes as a vice-presidential candidate to run with President Roosevelt for a second term. The secretary asked me to stop by his office to report on the progress made by my advisers at the Washington conference. When I finished my report, the secretary asked, "What are your advisers doing out there?" I replied that they were working long hours to get out grazing permits to qualified stockmen. "That's not what I mean," he said, pointing to himself. "What are they doing for me?"

I was speechless at this suggestion that the Taylor Grazing Act should be an instrument of political patronage. The secretary then pulled from his desk a large photograph of himself, made presumably for campaign purposes. Seeing my dismay, he put it back in his desk and abruptly ended the interview.

Farrington R. Carpenter (front row, fifth from right) stands with members of his advisory boards, along with Harold L. Ickes (seventh from right), and Ebert K. Burlew (sixth from right), assistant secretary to Ickes.

From that time on, the secretary ignored me, confining our relations to the exchange of formal letters. I learned from Burlew, however, that he was infuriated by an article about me entitled "Capitol Cowboy," which Robert McCormick wrote in a March 1938 issue of *Collier's Weekly.* It was a humorous piece in which McCormick described my hobby as picking off bureaucrats and added that the "starched-shirt flumdiddles of high society in Washington choked him." McCormick also had me saying that I found the "Capitol's bureaucracy a hard mule to ride" and that my Washington office was "so plush I couldn't find a place for my feet used to stirrups." I was told by Oscar Chapman that the secretary was particularly enraged because McCormick quoted me as saying that I had accepted the position on the understanding that the Taylor Grazing Act would be a decentralized administration.

In November 1938 all my district advisory board members came to Washington to celebrate the completion of the Federal Range Code, which provided for grazing permits under the terms of the grazing act. Soon after, Secretary Ickes asked me for my resignation and said that he had decided on a new director of the Grazing Division. I consulted with my Washington friend, Judge

Harold M. Stephens, who said that if I opposed resignation at the secretary's request, I was entitled to a hearing on any charges against me. He also said that I should not hand in a voluntary resignation without a letter from the secretary saying that my services had been satisfactory.

Fortified with this advice, I wrote out my resignation and took it to Ickes. He read it and said, "You haven't signed it."

"No," I said, "and I won't until you give me a letter stating that my services have been satisfactory."

"You'll wait a hell of a long time for that," he replied.

A week went by. Finally, Burlew called me to his office and said that the secretary had written me a good letter, but that he could not deliver it until he had my letter of resignation. Not trusting Burlew, I read the secretary's letter and found it to be satisfactory. Then I gave Burlew my letter of resignation.

When I said goodbye to Secretary Ickes, he remarked, "Now I'll put those advisory boards in their proper place." I knew what he meant and I knew that if he succeeded, it was the end of our experiment to put democratic procedures into the Taylor Grazing Act. I had walked nearly eighty feet to the secretary's desk in that long room of his. When I turned and started to walk out, he stood up behind his desk and yelled, "You're out of a job! You're out of a job!"

I did not look back.

FOURTEEN

Colorado's Tax Collector

I need not have feared in November 1938 that the pepperish curmudgeon would carry out his threat to put "those advisory boards in their proper place." In July 1939 Congress amended the Taylor Grazing Act in the following way to give my advisory boards permanent status: "There shall be an advisory board of local stockmen in each district, in order that the Secretary of the Interior may have the benefit of the fullest information and advice concerning physical, economic and other local conditions in the several grazing districts."

In 1946, when Secretary Ickes ended his thirteen-year reign as the boss of the "Department of Everything in General," the Grazing Service and the GLO were consolidated under President Truman into the huge Bureau of Land Management (BLM), charged with administering 457 million acres of surface land and mineral leases. The new organization retained my system of locally elected stockmen's advisory boards and grazing district boundaries.

After four years and five months as director of the Grazing Division, I was happy to get back with my family to our beautiful Dawson Ranch of registered Herefords. And in returning I found many changes in Hayden. Oil had been discovered in the Hamilton Dome near Craig, and the Texas Oil Company had built a refinery there. Craig had also become the largest shipping point for feeder lambs in the United States.

I kept my law office in Hayden but I had very little practice.

After being elected precinct committeeman for the Republican Party in the Hayden district, I spent much time politicking. We Republicans were a lean and hungry bunch in the 1930s, for the New Deal Democrats had taken up most of the offices. During the 1920s, however, I had come to know a young lawyer, Ralph L. Carr, who practiced in Antonito in the San Luis Valley. He had been born in the little Wet Mountain silver camp of Rosita, where his Scotch-Irish father had been a miner. Ralph was about my age and had received his law degree from the University of Colorado a year after I graduated from Harvard Law School. He and Lowell Thomas had been reporters together on the *Victor Daily Record* in Cripple Creek. In the 1930s Carr was an attorney for Conejos County while I was district attorney in my area.

Ralph had become an expert on Colorado interstate water matters, and we agreed on many issues. A plump, charming man, Ralph was always in a jovial mood and enjoyed having a good time, as I did. But, as I found out later, behind that cherubic countenance there was an iron will. Ralph was intransigently determined to do what he thought was right, whatever the consequences.

In 1938 the Colorado Republican leadership picked Ralph Carr to get the party out of its political doldrums by running him for governor of Colorado against an unexciting Democratic incumbent, Teller Ammons. Our Colorado senator, "Big Ed" Johnson from Craig, was a Democrat but rabidly anti–New Deal. We felt that Big Ed would give our man strong support, just as though he were a Democrat.

Ralph Carr was a superb campaigner. When he came to Hayden, I arranged for him to give a talk in the town hall. It was to be held in the evening, and I organized a torchlight procession to drum up attendance. The torches—cattails from the Yampa River dipped in gasoline—were carried by high school boys, who got so entranced in their job that they ran all over Hayden's side streets and alleys. It was a wonder they did not set the whole town on fire.

Our candidate won the governorship, and soon after his election Carr appointed me to a commission for the promotion of tourism in the state. Two years later he named me as Colorado's representative on the Interstate Water Commission. Meanwhile he was struggling to remedy a problem caused by New Deal depression legislation which required matching funds from state

sources to pay for new activities taken on by the federal government. To raise these funds, the Colorado legislature had enacted
a state income tax, a state sales tax, a motor fuel and vehicle tax,
and an increased gift and inheritance tax.

The collection of these taxes was assigned to the state treasurer, the state auditor, and the attorney general. Each of these
state agencies set up a little kingdom of its own, and there was no
overriding supervision to harmonize their activities. With the aid
of bipartisan support in the legislature, Governor Carr was able
to get a law passed on March 14, 1941, that provided for a new
state Department of Revenue combining all the state revenue-
collecting agencies under the authority of one director. The position, which paid a salary of $6,500, was considered a political
plum because the governor was paid only $5,000 a year, and no
mansion was provided for the governor's family.

On a pleasant June day in 1941, I picked up the mail and a
Denver newspaper from my box at the Hayden Post Office.
During my noon dinner, I read an article in the paper about the
new Administrative Code Act and Governor Carr's plan to appoint a director of revenue. While I was reading the news, my
telephone rang.

"Hello, Ferry. This is Ralph Carr."

"Hello, Governor. How are things under the capitol dome?"

"Fine. Just fine. But they'll be better when you take the appointment I'm about to offer you. Ferry, will you accept the
position of director of revenue? I need you in Denver to head the
department. We need somebody with your reputation of integri-
ty. I want you to start right away, as soon as you can. And I want
you to take the job."

What can a man say when the governor of his state asks him to
serve in just that way? I begged for time to consider. When I
hung up the phone, I did some fast thinking. There were
practical problems. I would have to move to Denver and forsake
my Hayden law practice. I was still the only resident lawyer
Hayden had ever had, and I would lose the close association I
had with my registered Hereford business. The cattle market in
1941 was in the low swing of its traditional seven-year cycle, and
I had a family and three youngsters to support. But the $6,500
salary looked big—and then there was my admiration for Ralph
Carr.

Ralph L. Carr, governor of Colorado from 1939 to 1943.

Even a casual reading of the Administrative Code Act made me realize that it was no ordinary piece of legislation. It was Governor Carr's answer to Colorado's most imperative need—sufficient revenue to operate the government. Two state senators of opposing political parties had pushed the act through the legislature—Robert G. Bosworth of Denver, a Republican, and Price Brisco of Idaho Springs, a Democrat. Governor Carr's director of revenue would head a new kind of facility that would be a model for state government everywhere. Putting it into operation looked like a real challenge for anyone with crusading instincts. I phoned Governor Carr the next day and accepted the appointment.

My experience as a bill collector was limited to representing my law clients and collecting pay for my bulls from hard-pressed cattlemen. But one of my grazing district advisers in Utah, Heber Bennion, had recently organized Utah's consolidated revenue department. I drove my Ford roadster to Salt Lake City, where Bennion took me through his offices and offered to loan me his chief clerk and auditor for a month to help me in setting up Colorado's new Department of Revenue.

Bennion advised me to get the help of James Martin, a professor at Kentucky State University. Martin was an authority on state taxation and had managed Kentucky's finances with great success. Before I could staff my new department, I formed a committee consisting of Bennion, Martin, and the heads of the old revenue agencies. We made a "blueprint" for the new operation and posted it in the hallway of the revenue department annex. It created a commotion, for it provided for a revenue staff of 157 fewer employees than had been employed by the former regimes.

The "blueprint" prompted a number of employees to picket the Capitol annex with banners and make soapbox speeches. The protest acquainted me with Colorado's peculiar method of employment. There were two kinds of employees—"certified" and "provisional," the latter chosen by the time-honored spoils system of political preferment.

I was anxious to get away from the rivalries of the old officeholders and bring in new blood—people who would inaugurate up-to-date revenue collection processes. The Administrative Code Act empowered me to appoint a chief of staff services to be my right hand in running the department. I went to Clem Collins, head of the School of Commerce at the University of Denver, to find such a chief. He recommended one of his graduate students, Harold Hurst, whom I appointed. But the Civil Service Commission had a favorite of its own for the job and refused to pay Hurst's salary. I appealed for help to two civic-minded Denver attorneys, W. W. Grant and Morrison Shafroth, who took my case to court without pay. District Judge Robert W. Steele upheld my appointment of Hurst and ordered the state treasurer to pay his salary.

It happened that on the day of my victory, I had promised to deliver a carload of Hereford bulls to a stockman in New Mexico. Governor Carr gave me the weekend off. When the bulls in the freight car reached Denver, I got a ride in the caboose behind them. I discovered that another passenger in the caboose was accompanying a carload of bananas bound for California. Whenever the freight train stopped, the banana man would run along the side of the train to take the temperature of his bananas, and I would follow him to see if my bulls were in good health. When the freight train reached La Junta, the banana man said goodbye, as his car was going west and mine south. He asked my name.

"Ferry Carpenter," I said.

"Heck," he said, "I know about you. You are that son of a bitch who is raising hell with the state government."

The banana man's remark may have led me to think that I ought to live up to his description of me. In any event, back in Denver on Monday I found on my desk a service-tax charge of twenty dollars due from Governor Carr when he received a state fee of a thousand dollars and had not paid the tax on it. Nobody had dared to try to collect it, so they dumped the problem on me.

I strode to Governor Carr's office and put the due bill on his desk.

"Why don't you pay your taxes, Ralph?" I asked.

"Oh, I paid that tax long ago," he replied.

"No, you didn't."

He called his secretary to check the matter. She could not find the receipt. When she returned after further searching, I said to the governor, "Why don't you pay up now and have it over with."

The governor reached for his checkbook.

"Wait a minute," I said. "Please add penalty and interest. They come to $6.48 more."

The governor was getting red in the face. "I thought the interest and penalty on the first offense was discretionary with the director. You don't mean to say that you're going to make me pay it?"

"I sure am," I said. "People have been dodging these taxes for seven years. If I knock off the penalty and interest for you, everybody will say I give personal favors."

Back in my office I set the governor's check on my desk. Later an old Larimer Street auctioneer, along with his attorney, came in begging to be let off a seven-year-old unpaid service tax. As the auctioneer laid his head on my desk and began to weep, his lawyer explained that the old man would be glad to pay the tax but wanted to be spared the penalty and interest.

I said to the lawyer, "You wouldn't want anything for your client that other citizens don't get, would you?"

"Oh, no," he replied. "We just feel that paying the penalty and interest is unfair."

"Governor Carr," I said, picking up the check, "signed *this* for tax, penalty, and interest, and he burst into tears, too. That's the way he was treated by this department when he failed to pay his tax."

The lawyer took the auctioneer by the arm. "Come on," he said, "let's go down to the cashier."

From the start of my revenue department appointment I knew that I needed the confidence of its three hundred employees, mostly women who ran the bookkeeping machines under the direction of some thirty male supervisors. To know my employees better, I made a practice of walking through the work rooms at 5:00 P.M. to chat with anybody who wanted to speak to me. One day a young woman asked if she could see me in my office. When we were alone, she said, "I've worked on the machines for some years with twenty-five other girls. My husband is in the army with the Eighty-ninth Division, and we have a small son. I work because his army paycheck isn't enough to support us. Now the department's picnic is coming up soon, and my supervisor wants to date me. He tells me to wear a silk dress with nothing underneath. You know what he means, Mr. Carpenter, and he says it will cost me my job if I turn him down."

I said that I would see what I could do about it.

The Civil Service Commission was hardly sympathetic when I tried to file charges with them against the offending supervisor. Women's rights were of no concern in 1941. The members of the commission explained that people at the state capitol had no time to waste on matters of private morality, and even the attorney general declined to prosecute the case. That brought out my stubborn streak. I decided to prosecute it myself. If one supervisor could get away with this, others would try the same sort of persuasion on my office women.

At the trial, the young woman told the story exactly as she had told it to me. The Civil Service Commission and the supervisor's lawyer had expected an easy acquittal, but her story impressed them both. During a recess, the defense lawyer asked me if I would dismiss the case if the supervisor resigned—and an agreement to that end was struck between both parties.

That ended the matter. The result got around the revenue department, and from then on I found nothing but smiles from the office women on my 5:00 P.M. tours.

Years later, as I was riding a bus to Denver, the driver said, "Aren't you Farrington Carpenter?"

"I am."

"I know you from news photos. I'm the husband of the girl you protected against the woman-chaser during the war. My wife wrote to me about what you did, and I've always wanted to thank you."

As the saying goes, you win some, you lose some.

When I moved to Denver to become director of revenue, I rented a little house on South University Boulevard. Then I bought a bicycle for the five-mile ride from my house to the capitol annex. Immediately, of course, I had to go to city hall to get a license for the bike. There I found myself in a long line of school children getting their licenses from a police sergeant, who never even looked up when I reached his table.

"What kinda bike you got?" he said.

"A Ranger."

"Do your parents approve of you riding a bicycle?"

When I didn't answer, he looked up.

"I haven't asked my parents," I said. "I was born in 1886."

He laughed and gave me a license.

On the way back to the office I ran into E. Ray Campbell, attorney for *The Denver Post*. I told him about getting my bike license, and he thought it was a good tale. Next day a *Post* photographer caught me on my bike at the statehouse, and the story of a state official riding five miles daily to work was published all over Colorado. Soon after that, when I gave a talk to the Walsenburg Chamber of Commerce, the table was decorated with a representation of me on a bicycle.

But my enthusiasm for bicycles came a cropper. Since the war effort had brought about gas rationing, I got the notion that all my thirty-five tax collectors should put their state cars in storage and make their rounds on bicycles. Governor Carr approved the idea. Meanwhile, however, my collectors heard that I planned to take away their cars and complained to the state purchasing agent. A person would have thought I had urged taking away their wives. It soon developed that all thirty-five collectors had hernias or sciatica or balance disability or other physical defects that made bike riding impossible. Thus, when the governor asked the state purchasing agent to buy thirty-five bicycles for the collectors, he received a blunt refusal.

Calling me to his office one day, the governor said, "I have a decision to make. I either have to lose my purchasing agent or my director of revenue. Which is it to be?"

"Forget it," I said. "I'm not going to make an issue of the bicycles."

The time to be stubborn is when you know you can win.

As director of revenue, I spent a good deal of time finding products that had escaped taxation. I discovered, for instance, that Colorado newspapers paid no sales tax on newsprint and ink. When I notified the Colorado Press Association that I intended to tax these purchases, Jack Foster, the editor of the *Rocky Mountain News*, refused to pay the tax and William C. Shepherd, publisher of *The Denver Post*, was greatly disturbed. Nevertheless, I decided to levy the new tax and take the newspapers to court if they failed to pay.

The attorney general, however, disliked the scheme. "I won't go to court for you, Carpenter," he said. "You start to tax those fellows who have never been taxed and you'll have big trouble." As it turned out, I did not have to go to court, for the newspaper people dodged the issue. They went to the legislature and got the law amended so that sales and purchases of newsprint and printer's ink were deemed to be wholesale sales exempt from taxation.

This defeat did not keep me from continuing to search for collectible sales taxes. I next learned that morticians were not paying sales tax on the coffins they sold. When the State Association of Morticians heard of my plan to tax them, they sent an official to explain that instead of coffins, they sold a "service" to the family of the deceased.

The morticians' society invited me to join them for a dinner at the Shirley-Savoy Hotel, which was attended by all the practitioners in Colorado. During the dinner, the morticians begged off the sales tax on coffins, saying that their margin of profit was so low that they had a hard time just staying in business. I asked for some examples of why they were losing money, and one of them told me that undertakers did not get a big enough fee for conducting a funeral for "ship-ins."

"What are ship-ins?" I asked.

"A ship-in," he replied solemnly, "is a deceased person buried in Colorado who died in another state. The out-of-state mortician receives a fee for preparing the body for shipment, and the Colorado mortician who receives the body gets only a minor part of the fee for funeral expenses."

"Don't you make it up on your ship-outs?" I asked.

"No," he said. "There aren't so many people dying in Colorado as in other states. We get mostly ship-ins. The ship-outs are few and far between."

Then he made another point. The morticians had big extra expenses by having to maintain an "eternal light."

"What's an eternal light?" I asked.

"We have to keep a light going all night long in the room where the deceased is kept before burial because people don't like to think of their departed loved ones resting in the dark." Though the "eternal light" was simply a forty-watt lamp, it was an expense, I was told, that could not be recovered by direct charge.

After the dinner, the president of the morticians' society thanked me for attending. I then shook hands with several of the morticians who looked me in the eye gloomily and said, "I hope I may meet you again."

A statewide audit conducted by my office later showed that the state's morticians were doing well. I therefore tacked seven years of back sales taxes, in addition to penalty and interest, on their current tax bills. As a result, tax collections took a big jump, and the monthly old-age pension checks benefited from this new source of revenue.

By now people around Denver were calling me the meanest man in Colorado, and the next effort of that meanest man was to expand the collection of service taxes imposed on those who performed personal services—dentists, doctors, lawyers, everybody. However, when we tried to collect this 2 percent service tax from lawyers, they all declared that it was unconstitutional. They were sure that the courts would protect them from what they considered unjust taxation.

At that time the Ernst and Cranmer Building in Denver was filled with lawyers. I told my collectors to start on the top floor and collect from every lawyer on down to the basement. If any of them took his case to court, we would thrash it out.

Every lawyer in the Ernst and Cranmer Building protested the tax, but most of them paid for fear I would make off with their office equipment. Those who refused to pay promised to take their case to the Colorado Supreme Court. I realized that to establish a test case I needed to go far from Denver where the lawyers could not gang up on me. As it turned out, one of my collectors operated near the Kansas state line. He was having trouble collecting the service tax from a lawyer there who felt safe from the tax because he was both Republican county chairman and a friend of Governor Carr. I told this collector to make a test case out of that eastern plains lawyer and to levy a "distraint" (seizure for debt) on him. The collector did not want to do it. "In all my seven years of collecting taxes," he said, "I've never done a distraint. How do I distrain?"

I explained it to him. "When you distrain you have the right to take any property in the delinquent's custody—whether his personal property or somebody else's—if he uses it in his business or profession. For instance, if the delinquent is a woodworker and makes storm windows and claims that his saws are owned by a hardware store, the saws are good for the tax and you can take them. Now you go ahead and levy on this lawyer."

The next morning the collector phoned me. He was very upset. "I went up to see that attorney," he said. "I told him I was sorry but I had orders from you personally to distrain if he wouldn't pay the tax. He said he wouldn't pay it. So I picked up one of his typewriters and took it to my car. Then I went back and picked up a copy of the *Statutes of Colorado* and another book on his desk. He followed me downstairs to the street protesting that the typewriter belonged to his stenographer and the statute book belonged to the county commissioners. The other book, *The Life and Trial of Jesus Christ*, belonged to the public library. He said that if I went off with property that wasn't mine he would have me arrested for stealing."

I told my distressed collector, "That's just dandy. You have an ironclad defense for everything you did. Taxes come first!" When I hung up my phone rang again. It was Governor Carr.

"Ferry," he said, "why do you always pick out our biggest party supporters to test your tax laws?"

"They're *your* tax laws, Governor, not mine," I said.

Then both of us had a good laugh about it. And eventually the eastern Colorado lawyer paid his tax.

When the county treasurers of Colorado held their annual convention in Colorado Springs, I made it a point to attend. All sixty-three of them were complaining that, unlike real-estate taxes, it was difficult collecting personal-property taxes. I had studied this problem and remembered my success in 1929 selling bulls by way of the silver screen. I therefore had my revenue people make a short movie featuring a typical county treasurer answering the questions of a taxpayer. Although it lacked the drama of cattle crossing the flooded Yampa River, the film had some appeal. In it a treasurer explained how taxes served the home folks, the needy, and the young.

I told the treasurers that my department would furnish the film on request, and they could have it shown gratis at their local movie theaters as a public service. For ten dollars, we would also flash their smiling faces on the screen for them to use as vote getters at election time. At the convention the county treasurers were enthusiastic about the idea and thereafter kept us busy sending them films that included their portraits.

After I had served as director of revenue for about eight months I made a report of our activities to the legislature. It showed that we had reduced the number of employees by 23 percent, reduced the cost of collection by 20.8 percent, and increased the revenue collected by 6.8 percent. Then, in December 1941, Pearl Harbor was bombed, and whatever progress we had made was of no consequence as the country plunged into war with Japan. Indignation against the Japanese swept the land. In California the army herded all Japanese, whether citizens or not, into concentration camps.

It was on this issue of the camps that Ralph Carr showed his heroic stature as the noblest of Colorado governors. Though he knew that his political future was at stake, he issued a proclamation inviting the ostracized Japanese to come to Colorado. At a meeting of western state leaders on the matter at Salt Lake City, he was alone in volunteering to accept the Japanese, arguing that they had the same rights as all other Americans. Thus, in September 1942, more than a thousand frightened, homesick Japanese families were hauled to a flimsy cardboard city called Amache near Granada in eastern Colorado. A storm of protest swirled around them among the beet-pickers along the Arkansas River, who feared that the Japanese would cause their wages to be lowered. Former members of the Ku Klux Klan—who had brought disgrace to Colorado in 1924 by ensuring the election of a Klansman, Clarence J. Morley, as governor—once again donned white sheets, this time against the "yellow peril."

While the protesters denounced Governor Carr, he stood by the Japanese. When his four-year term as governor ended in 1943, he ran for the United States Senate against the incumbent, "Big Ed" Johnson, who side-stepped the Japanese issue. Carr was defeated and resumed his private law practice. Seven years later he returned to politics, running for governor against a Democrat, Walter W. Johnson. In August 1950, with victory seemingly assured, Carr bruised an ankle in Grand Junction. Infection set in and he died in Denver at the age of sixty-two, campaigning vigorously to the end from his hospital bed.

Carr had been replaced as governor in 1943 by the Republican stalwart John F. Vivian. Since Governor Vivian wanted his own man as director of revenue, my term of office ended with Governor Carr's. In any case, Vivian asked me to come and see him.

"Ferry," he said, "I have to send in nominees for your office. As you know, you have stirred up opposition. You've done a fine job, but the state senate will not confirm you. So just tell me that you don't want to submit your name to the senate."

Outside the governor's office I ran into Stephen Hart, a state senator and a Democrat.

"Steve," I said, "Governor Vivian tells me that the senate Democrats will oppose my confirmation as director of revenue."

"That's not so," Steve said. "The Democrats will support you."

"If that's true," I said, "I won't resign."

Steve was right. The Democrats did support me. But Governor Vivian gave me no support whatsoever, and I lost confirmation in the senate by one vote. It was cast by a Republican senator, Charlie Collins, who opposed me because I had worked for President Roosevelt and the New Deal.

As Eunice and I packed up to head for Hayden and home, I wondered if there was a jinx connected with the words "tax collector." I recalled Saint Matthew, who had collected taxes for the Romans on the camel route to Damascus. The job had made him a despised publican and a social outcast. But Saint Matthew left us the New Testament's finest account of the lessons of Jesus. If he could survive the shame of being a tax collector, perhaps there was hope for me.

FIFTEEN

Fund Raising for DU

After my tax collecting stint in Denver, Eunice and I spent an idyllic year doing what both of us loved best—raising purebred Hereford cattle on our Yampa River ranch near Hayden. But our rustic idyll was interrupted in late 1943 when a letter came to me from Morrison Shafroth, the well-known Denver lawyer. Eunice and I had seen a lot of the Shafroths in Washington and again in Denver, when Shafroth and his law partner, Will Grant, helped me in the court battles of the state revenue department.

Shafroth was president of the University of Denver's board of trustees. In his letter he asked me to move to Denver again to survey the finances of that venerable institution. At the time my cattle business was in a downswing, and Hayden was a very quiet place. I could not resist accepting another challenge.

My feeling toward the University of Denver had always been touched with nostalgia. It had been established by John Evans as a Methodist institution in 1864. First known as Colorado Seminary, it was renamed the University of Denver in 1880. My hometown of Evanston, Illinois, had been named for Evans in 1851, the year in which he had founded Northwestern University there. Achieving his wealth through investments in Chicago real estate, Evans was also a pillar of the Methodist church. Though the Carpenters were staunch Congregationalists, my family admired him, particularly when Abraham Lincoln sent him to Denver in 1862 as Colorado's second territorial governor.

Although I never met John Evans—who died in Denver in

1897—during my childhood in Evanston, my parents always spoke of him in reverent tones. When the Carpenter children picnicked near the site of the large Evans home on the lakefront, I imagined his ghost striding about—a ponderous eminence resembling the prophet Moses with a long, thick beard. In later years my childhood awe of Evans was transferred to his progeny, who dominated the Denver business and social scene. His son, William Gray Evans, had worked heroically and artfully to induce the state of Colorado to build the Moffat Tunnel. When W. G. Evans died in 1924, the mantle of what my friends called "the Evans fiefdom over Denver" passed to his grandson, also named John Evans.

Eunice and I admired still another Evans, John Evans's daughter Anne. When the Peter McFarlane family gave the Central City Opera House to the University of Denver, Anne used all the prestige of the Evans name to bring about the Central City Opera Festival. The festival became famous nationally for alcoholic revelry amid the clangor of slot machines. In the Teller House bar, Eunice and I wondered what the austere John Evans would have thought of his daughter's boisterous recreation at Central City in the name of his Methodist university of Denver.

When I arrived in Denver for my new job early in 1944, I was given a briefing by Carl Feiss, director of DU's School of Architecture and Planning. Feiss had just been asked by the board of trustees to present a plan for centering a second campus around the downtown Civic Center. At that time the university's main campus in University Park consisted of the Graduate School, the College of Liberal Arts, the School of Science and Engineering, the Department of Social Work, and the independent Iliff School of Theology. Other schools, however, were scattered about in the downtown area some five miles away. The School of Commerce, Accounts, and Finance was located in an old building at Twentieth and Glenarm ("a pet slum," Feiss called it), and the Law School had just been evicted from the second floor of Mapelli's Butcher Shop at Fifteenth and Cleveland Place, where for years future attorneys had learned the rules of equity while surrounded by the aroma of fresh sausage and bacon. The Division of Fine Arts was also located downtown, in Chappell House near the state capitol on Logan Street. About four thousand students were enrolled in all these schools.

I continued my education by discussing financial problems with the university's chancellor, Ben Cherrington, a charming, broad-gauged man who had experience in just about everything—from football coaching to international relations. By 1944 the United States had been at war for more than two years, and the need for military men was so great that the number of male students at the university had been reduced. The loss of their tuitional revenue was particularly painful to the university because almost 78 percent of its total income was from tuition, compared to an average of 55 percent at most colleges. This posed the threat of the university's being closed or turned into a female seminary. To meet that threat, Shafroth and his trustees had hired me to survey the situation.

The recent announcement of a gift of $20 million to Northwestern University in Evanston had alerted the trustees to the possibility of other sources of income to supplement the lost tuitional revenue. Having been raised in the shadow of Northwestern University, I thought that a visit to my hometown was an ideal way to find out how that school had gone about raising all those millions. I went first to Northwestern's treasurer, Harry Wells, who explained how the university had decided to eradicate the unfriendliness that often existed between universities and the communities in which they were located.

Wells told me that a Chicago banker named Melvin S. Traylor had been elected president of Northwestern's board in 1930. Traylor went to work at once to bring Northwestern and the community closer together. He invited 150 of the city's leading citizens to form a group known as the Associates of Northwestern University. This group became an advisory agency to the board of trustees on all matters affecting the future of the university. Traylor also discontinued the traditional once-a-year alumni campaign for donations to offset deficits in the budget. Instead he put the personnel used in those alumni drives into a new agency called the Department of Development. It was charged with conducting a year-round effort to get contributions to Northwestern and to do so in a businesslike way. Traylor's innovations during the next eleven years were so successful that the university's endowment fund had been increased from $5.5 million to over $70 million. Its earnings alone were enough to offset the loss in male tuitional income caused by the war.

To acquaint me with Northwestern's Department of Development, Wells sent me to Thomas Gonser, its director. Gonser had
the title of vice-president, a yearly salary of $12,000, two assis-
tants at $5,000 each, and an office staff of six clerks. He also had
the fervor of a good life insurance agent. Opening a drawer in his
desk, Gonser showed me a card index containing the names of
six thousand wealthy people who lived within a radius of a hundred miles of the university.

"You have to find out where the money is if you want to get
it," he told me. He said that he had obtained the names from
published lists of big taxpayers as well as determining the names
of owners of expensive automobiles from their license tags. He
took me into a room where his clerks were working on a high
pile of newspapers containing the names of Illinois people who
had won lotteries or had received substantial divorce settlements,
salary bonuses, or other large transfers of money. Gonser then
showed me copies of letters sent to all prospective donors telling
them how their gifts would be spent by the university and how
they would qualify for deductions on their income-tax returns.
The letter offered donors free advice in making their wills and
the help of a tax expert on their returns. The department had all
the research equipment of a modern collection agency.

From Gonser I learned that many other educational institutions had adopted similar ways of attracting gifts and legacies.
He advised me to visit the University of Chicago, where I subsequently became acquainted with the Chicago University Civic
Sponsors, an organization similar to the Associates of
Northwestern University. Chicago's director of development
showed me how he kept in touch with several hundred not-
for-profit foundations which were headquartered in New York
City. I studied the list and noted that three of them were in Denver and two in Colorado Springs. None of them had ever been
solicited by DU.

I went next to the Illinois Institute of Technology, which had
formerly been known as Armour Institute after its founder, Phil-
lip D. Armour, the wealthy meat packer. Occupying a unique position in the relationship of industry and science, this institution
provided laboratories and testing machines for the industries of
the Chicago area and provided advice by faculty scientists of the
institute. It had a scale of fees for addressing long-term problems
requiring research. If a manufacturer wanted an investigation

made, for instance, he could have the yearly services of a graduate fellow for $2,500. The industry was billed every month for the faculty member's work in addition to use of the institute's machines. This program produced funds for the institute far beyond expectations, and its help was so much in demand that in the early years of World War II it was able to erect a new $1.25 million laboratory with funds from its service to Chicago businesses.

In talking with James Almond, president of a large professional fund-raising firm, I also learned that money was easy to get for the Illinois Institute of Technology because, as he put it, "When you ask someone for a dime, he's glad to give it if he has already received fifteen cents worth of help from you." Almond pointed out that the Chicago manufacturers who paid money to the institute charged it as a business expense on their tax returns or showed it as a deductible contribution for educational purposes.

In addition, I was fortunate to meet a man identified with a new development in the field of private funds for public institutions—George Haight. A Chicago patent attorney, Haight was an alumnus of the University of Wisconsin and had organized what was known as the Wisconsin Foundation. To this foundation all inventions and scientific discoveries made by the faculty of the University of Wisconsin were assigned. The foundation then undertook to patent and commercialize them, giving the inventor a 15 percent royalty on the net proceeds. The other profits went to the university to improve its research activity. One of the Wisconsin professors isolated vitamin D in 1925 by the use of ultraviolet rays. The foundation patented this discovery and licensed the Quaker Oats Company to commercialize it. The foundation also patented D Con, a rat-poisoning formula that became popular and profitable. In this manner the foundation raised more than $8 million for the university's use.

Returning to Denver from Chicago, I put all the fund-raising information that I had collected into a preliminary report to the board of trustees on March 15, 1944. I recommended that DU follow procedures that Northwestern had used successfully and form a group of local citizens to be known as the Associates of Denver University. The board responded to my report by employing me on a full-time basis to serve the university as director of development. I was to operate under Chancellor Cherrington to modernize methods for getting gifts and grants to increase the university's endowment fund. I suggested next that the university's widespread activities be coordinated with a new, second campus augmenting the University Park campus on South University Boulevard. This new campus would adjoin Denver's downtown Civic Center.

Since the board's reaction to my work so far was favorable, I settled down to the job of surrounding myself with people who would make the Department of Development a success. Especially helpful from the start was Charles Greene, superintendent of Denver's public schools and a DU board member. Greene's particular interest was in increasing DU's enrollment by attracting more Denver high school graduates to its doors. He complained that no member of the DU faculty had visited a Denver public school in the past ten years. He called my attention to the work being done at Emily Griffith's famed Opportunity School to teach people how to better their status in industry. Greene felt that DU could attract students by offering similar training.

Soon after I began work, I found a person who knew everything there was to know about how DU operated—Evelyn Hosmer. Chancellor Cherrington's private secretary, she had served every chancellor before him from the regime of the legendary Henry Augustus Buchtel, who had saved DU from becoming a glue factory by foreclosure around the turn of the century. It was through the devoted work of Miss Hosmer that I was able to staff the new Department of Development and get it functioning. For legal aid I had Gordon O. Johnston, dean of the Law School. For planning I had Carl Feiss, formerly on the staff of the Denver Planning Commission. Ed Whittlesey was publicity chief and Randolph P. McDonough was director of DU Alumni Relations.

Fifteen months after my first report to the trustees, urging again the formation of the Associates of Denver University, John Evans, grandson of Colorado's territorial governor, organized the Associates. Evans and his committee sent out invitations to one hundred of Denver's leaders and their wives to attend a dinner at the University Club. I presided at the dinner. Those present responded enthusiastically to the idea of an expanded future and a second Civic Center campus for the university. Only one matter was left to be decided and that was who would be named chairman of the Associates. Everyone agreed that the ideal person for the position was Charles C. Gates, president of the Gates Rubber Company, the largest manufacturing plant in Denver. Since at that time Gates was on vacation in Acapulco, Mexico, the trustees asked me to go there and offer him the position.

I took a plane to Mexico City and from there phoned Gates, whom I had never met, at his Acapulco hotel. I asked for an appointment.

"I'm sorry, Mr. Carpenter," he said, "that you didn't phone me before you came down here. The only way to get from Mexico City to Acapulco is by air, and the reservations are all spoken for weeks ahead. Besides," he added, "if you got here, you couldn't find a place to stay."

Gates, of course, know nothing of what I had learned about getting anywhere and sleeping anywhere during hundreds of thousands of miles of travel for the Grazing Division all over the wild West. In any event, a good road ran 267 miles from Mexico City to Acapulco, and I found a driver and an old Pierce Arrow with a big back seat to sleep in. In Acapulco, I phoned Gates at his fashionable hotel, and he invited me to have dinner with him. After dinner we walked down to the beach to watch divers jump for coins from a high cliff into an ocean pool below.

Gates told me some of his history as a rubber manufacturer. He said that he had been a traveling salesman for some years. When his wife objected to his being away from home so much, he gave up selling and bought a small bicycle store and repair shop in Denver. While busy with bicycles, he started the Colorado Tire and Leather Company in 1911, making horse halters and leather tire covers. Seeing a brighter future in automobile accessories, he invented a rubber V-belt for cars and tires and retreads. No tires were made in Denver because of high freight rates, which kept heavy industries out of mile-high Denver. Gates renamed his business the Gates Rubber Company, bought options on factory sites, made agreements with labor unions, and asked the railroads to reduce their tariffs so that Denver could compete on the open market. The railroads saw his point and reduced their charges.

But Gates would not accept the chairmanship of the Associates. He said that he had tried once before to interest the board of trustees in improving the university's curriculum and had found that it was dominated by tight-fisted, old-guard bankers who would never spend $1.00 unless they could see a $1.50

return in a reasonable time. "That attitude toward spending never succeeds in promotional work," he said.

I returned to Denver and met with the board of trustees in the old Denver Club building. I told them all that Gates had said in his pessimistic appraisal of expanding DU and his view of the community's financial timidity. There was a tense silence when I finished my report. Then Henry C. Van Schaack, a new trustee and a prominent realtor, took the floor and said that he agreed with Gates. The university would have to take risks to accomplish anything, he said, adding that whenever the university got any money it was spent on the University Park campus, while the only place that made a profit was the downtown School of Commerce, Accounts, and Finance, housed in Carl Feiss's "pet slum." Van Schaack proposed an immediate campaign to raise money for a new School of Commerce building. Frank Ricketson, Jr., another new trustee, seconded Van Schaack's remarks, and soon the whole board fell to making plans and naming fund-raising committees for a new School of Commerce near the city's Civic Center.

Thomas A. Dines, a trustee and one of Denver's most civic-minded citizens, concocted a slogan for the drive: You can't have a great city without a great university. Several large donations were secured in advance of the well-planned campaign, and these were announced at times when the campaign lagged. One advance gift was of $50,000 from DU's "Lady Bountiful," Mrs. Verner Z. Reed. Her late husband had been paid a million-dollar commission for selling a Cripple Creek gold mine to an English company. Previously she had given the university its handsome Mary Reed Library and the Margery Reed Mayo Building, which housed Campton Bell's School of Theatre.

A campaign brochure was distributed showing how the expanded university was needed to encourage large industries to locate in Denver. All of us gave talks at the noon service clubs. The newspapers were supplied with daily reports of progress. In a short time $2 million was pledged and a new chapter began for DU in an active role to promote Denver's growth and prosperity.

While the campaign was going on, the Congress of the United States, under the leadership of my former boss, President Franklin D. Roosevelt, enacted a "rehabilitation act" for veterans, the G.I. Bill of Rights—so called because the words "general issue"

Farrington rises to speak at a DU banquet. Others at the table are Dr. Alfred C. Nelson (left), E. Grosvenor Plowman, and Robert Selig.

were used in military vernacular. The act provided for four years of college education or vocational training for qualified veterans who were wounded or had a disability. The government paid tuition up to $500 and charges for books and fees, plus a living expense of $50 a month for single veterans and $75 a month for veterans with dependents. Soon the G.I. bill was amended to include all veterans, whether or not wounded or disabled, and tuition payments were allowed in excess of the $500 limit. Living expenses were raised to $65 and $90. Almost overnight, admissions officers of every higher education facility in the land were besieged with applicants for admission.

This dramatic turn of events solved DU's tuitional revenue problem for the time being but created a new one—how to find facilities to handle the increased enrollments. In this new work, the Department of Development became an agency for the purchase of land. Space was needed for the new School of Commerce as well as for Quonset huts acquired from the Federal Housing Agency and trailers for the students near the University Park campus.

The site selected for the School of Commerce, Accounts, and Finance was near the intersection of Fifteenth Street and Cleveland Place, at the northern boundary of Denver's Civic Center. The Colorado State Capitol with its gleaming gold dome was at the east end of the center; the white crescent of the Denver City and County Building was on the west; and the Denver Public Library was on the south. In between was the pride of every Denverite—a spacious park of lawns, trees, walks, and esplanades, filled with memorials, bronze statues, and swarms of hungry pigeons. I had suggested this site to the board partly for its beauty and partly because it was close to the Civic Center, for I theorized that the city and county of Denver would find itself paying for much of the upkeep of DU's Civic Center campus.

One end of Cleveland Place, where a filling station sat, belonged to the F. G. Bonfils estate, which owned *The Denver Post*, the region's largest and most powerful newspaper. The other end was occupied by Mapelli's Butcher Shop on property leased to Mapelli's by the John Evans family. To get the filling station lots, Henry Van Schaack took me to call on Helen Bonfils, who, since the death of her father in 1933, virtually ran the *Post*. She was tall, blonde, and gaily energetic—and though she loved acting on the New York stage above all, she was devoted to DU. Like the families of John Evans, Charles Gates, and Lawrence Phipps, she was a strong supporter of Denver's cultural affairs. She promised at once to donate the Cleveland Place filling station lots if the Evans family would donate the Mapelli property on the other end—which they did. (Some years later, the Evans family gave the university funds to move, stone by stone, the beautiful Evans Methodist Chapel near the south side of the Civic Center to the University Park campus. John Evans had built the chapel in 1878 as a memorial to his daughter, Josephine Evans Elbert, the wife of Colorado's sixth territorial governor, who died of consumption in 1868. The lots where the chapel stood were also given by John Evans to the university.)

Elated with the acquisition of such priceless property, I went to see Carl Feiss, whose office overlooked the block where the new downtown campus was to be. When I told him of Helen Bonfils's generosity, he led me to the window. "Don't go after a lot or two on the fronting street only," he said. "Nobody gets excited over small enterprises. Tell the newspaper that the University of Denver is taking over the whole square block and will put a building on it which will be the most modern school of commerce in the United States. In that way the imagination of prospective donors will be stirred and they will want to particpate in the grandeur of it."

I reported Carl's advice to the trustees, who all agreed to enlarge the plan and acquire the whole of the city's Block 42. That would include the old four-story Monroe Hotel on the corner and several boardinghouses and small hotels. The university had two advantages in buying privately owned buildings in the block: first, owners of the property were inclined to sell because they did not like the idea of running businesses near a campus, and second, property owned by DU was exempt from property taxation, which protected campus property put up as security in future purchases. With these advantages, DU was able to buy all the buildings in the block with a small down payment and a long-term balance of payments secured by the property.

From 1944 on, I spent a good deal of time on the road raising funds for DU among alumni in outlying towns. I had a pleasant companion on these motor trips, Randolph McDonough, who was director of Alumni Relations. We attended alumni dinners by the score and consumed chicken croquettes by the ton. We stopped anywhere that had as many as two or three alumni to set up dinners—all those charming eastern plains towns like Yuma, Holyoke, and Kit Carson and the cities of Sterling, Lamar, and Trinidad. Crossing the Continental Divide, we begged for money in Grand Junction, Durango, Gunnison, and Meeker. Chancellor Cherrington fronted for us often. When he was tied up, Randolph and I put on the show. As we bumped along, I would practice a story on Randy, and if he failed to smile I would drop it and try another. Our biggest trouble was keeping the car running. Because of the recent war, only poor retread tires were available, and we found ourselves having to fix blow-outs every ten miles or so. We chewed gum constantly, using it to plug holes in leaky radiators. In spite of our troubles on that alumni campaign, Randolph and I raised $2 million.

Back in Denver, work on the new Civic Center campus went along steadily. As the School of Commerce building began to go up, I remember Evelyn Hosmer lugging in her typewriter—ignoring wet paint and hammering—to take letters for Carl Feiss, Gordon Johnston, and me. Evelyn stuck by us and saved us whenever we said the wrong things to the right people, or vice versa.

Gordon Johnston started work there still wearing his resplend-
ent Navy uniform, which soon got covered with plaster dust.
Since we were lawyers, Gordon and I had to handle the eviction
of tenants in the new buildings purchased by the university. I remember serving notice on a manager of one of the four transient
hotels which we took over. She was a tough little old woman
with an unprintable vocabulary, and she carried a gun under her
skirt to repel unruly roomers. She told me fondly of earlier days
of glory when she ran two successful parlor houses in the gold
camp at Victor before retiring to Denver to run her respectable
establishment adjoining the Civic Center. One day, as Gordon
and I examined her place, we found a secret gambling den with a
trap-door entrance in the alley under Marian Buchan's sculpture
studio.

Years later, reading a letter of reminiscences that I received
from Carl Feiss, I recalled that there were no electric lights in the
cellar at 211 Fifteenth Street, and we used matches to light our
way through tons of scenery belonging to Campton Bell's Little
Theatre. Frequently we saw rats whose eyes gleamed from
behind the props of Macbeth and other of Bell's productions.
Carl's letter also described a cold winter morning when the new
girl's dorm opened at the corner of Fifteenth and Court Place and
the girls found themselves without heat or hot water. Carl ran in
and stoked the furnace himself. "I suppose," he wrote, "that I
was the highest paid janitor DU ever had, though the University
has never been known for high salaries."

The G.I. Bill of Rights had temporarily solved our problem of
tuition from male students, but it was not a permanent cure. In
looking around to see what other colleges were doing about the
problem, I found something that was new to me. In 1928 the Nebraska legislature had passed an act that empowered cities to
vote on the establishment and maintenance of a university—in
this case, Omaha Municipal University. I described the Nebraska
act to the DU board, which appointed a city-wide committee on
March 15, 1945, to consider municpal support for DU. To get
something started, John Evans, Tom Dines, Morrison Shafroth,
and I called on Mayor Ben Stapleton. We found the mayor to be
receptive to the idea, but he advised us to have the matter
brought up to him by the Denver City Council. Following the
mayor's suggestion, I interviewed each council member and
found that all of them favored municipal support of DU by schol-

arships paid for by the city and given to qualified graduates of Denver high schools.

To promote our municipal scholarship plan, I wrote a guest editorial for *The Denver Post* in which I tried to show how DU could be expanded to take care of junior college work as well as to furnish technical and scientific help for employees of Denver's growing industries.

There was at this time dissatisfaction with Denver's city and county charter and a movement was under way to have it amended by popular vote to permit municipal scholarships. But the proposal to change the charter contained a number of controversial matters. As a result, our proposal for municipal support of DU received little attention. When the election was held on November 13, 1947, the proposed changes in the charter were defeated by a vote of 32,607 to 26,437.

Though our failure to win municipal support for DU was a disappointment, I was more than satisfied with the success of our four-year effort to raise funds and to urbanize DU by the creation of the Civic Center campus. I was also pleased that my plan of a research division with the university to solicit projects from government and private industry brought about the establishment of the Institute of Industrial Research, renamed Denver Research Institute, with an annual program of contract research exceeding $6.2 million.

However, in 1948 I felt that I had completed my task as DU's director of development. Once again Eunice and I yearned to leave the city and cross the Continental Divide to our rambling ranch home near Hayden. I tendered my resignation to the board of trustees. My parting act was to give them a sixty-six-page report summarizing the achievements of the past four exciting years. The board honored me by electing me one of its members, and I served as such until 1952.

SIXTEEN

More Beef for Less Money

As always, Eunice and I found it refreshing to return to Hayden after my fund-raising adventure at DU. For her own part, Eunice had taken a lively part in Denver activities, serving as president of the Denver League of Women Voters. Back in Hayden I had leisure to collect material for the autobiography that I planned to write some day. I spent little time now in my Hayden law office because my partner, Fred Videon, moved our joint practice to Craig shortly after World War II. In 1946 we were joined by Jim Mosely, and the firm name became Carpenter, Videon and Mosely. Largely through their efforts we had an excellent practice.

Fred was far more than a law partner. He was my close friend and alter ego. Born in Denver, he had come to Hayden in 1929 fresh out of Harvard and the DU Law School. He was Hayden's town attorney in 1933 when we combined our practices. Fred had a delightful dry wit and a scholar's love of law which dovetailed neatly with my own feelings about the profession. Fred really ran our law firm in Craig. I did counseling but the court work we left to Jim.

With time on my hands, I became in the early 1950s one of the founders of Performance Registry International, a long-overdue method of evaluating cattle by the condition of the carcass after butchering. It had been the practice of the American Hereford Association and the other breed groups to judge cattle by the way they looked when alive in the stock show ring. Registration

LEFT: *Evan G. Marr, Vermonter, cowman, banker, and manager, about 1956.* BELOW: *Carpenter and longtime law partner Fred A. Videon, at Ferry's ninetieth birthday, August 10, 1976.*
OPPOSITE PAGE
TOP: *George ("Scotty") Annand with Onward Pioneer, about 1942.* BOTTOM: *Evan Marr, Scotty Annand, and Ferry shortly after leasing the Dawson Ranch, about 1926.*

papers as evidence of special worth were issued only to animals with pedigrees consisting of long lines of notable ancestors.

My involvement with Performance Registry dated back to 1922, when Jack White and I were ranching on our homesteads at Elkhead. As we worked to upgrade our purebred Herefords, we found it impossible to improve our herd on the unfenced open range using our first fine breeding bull, old Beau Blanchard 64th, because lesser bulls from the big commercial outfits nearby kept wandering into our cow herd.

Jack and I joined the American Hereford Association in 1910 and in 1922 entered some of our registered Hereford yearlings at the Denver stock show. But we came to shun the show ring and the propaganda and huckstering which it generated. We were quite sure by then that the Hereford was the best of all beef cattle because of its ability to rustle for food in a climate of heavy snowfall like ours. We admired it also for the larger quantity of milk that the mother cows produced for their calves. But we could not fully swallow the credo of the Hereford people that outside appearance and pedigree were the only reliable factors for evaluating an animal. We could recall a comparison that was made in 1908 at the Chicago Livestock Exposition between blue ribbon winners judged "on the hoof"—in the show ring—and their carcasses when judged "on the hook" in the cooler of the packer. The comparison showed that there was no correlation between the two. As a matter of fact, in over forty years of recording such comparisons there were seventy-three times when the high-placed carcasses were of animals that got no placing at all in the "on-hoof" visual inspections at the stock shows.

With these results in mind, Jack and I made it a habit to urge customers to look for the red meat inside our bulls and to disregard their pedigrees or the color of hair on their backs or the mottling on their faces. Jack and I favored long-legged, long-bodied, growthy bulls in the days when many buyers were unwilling to break loose from the lure of the purple ribbons of the stock show prize winners.

In 1925 Jack White left me to manage a big spread in North Park. I took the opportunity to lease the Dawson Ranch on the Yampa River. At the same time I installed modern electricity and plumbing into the old John B. Dawson ranch house (composed of five homestead cabins joined together). Then I moved Eunice and the children into it from Oak Point.

I had the good luck in 1926 to employ as operator of the business end of the ranch Evan Marr, who had been working at the H. W. Gossard Ranch in Axial Basin south of Craig. Then George ("Scotty") Annand joined me as my herdsman. When Scotty took over the breeding program at the Carpenter Ranch, my career as a Hereford breeder began in earnest, for he was regarded throughout northwestern Colorado as the ultimate authority on cattle quality. He was the rare kind of expert who could eyeball an animal and say, "That one will sire fine calves"—and sure enough, the calves would turn out that way. What Scotty based his judgment on was a mystery to me. I had to put it down to intuition, like a painter's eye for composition. For one thing, Scotty had a phenomenal memory. At our ranch he could tell us which bull a cow had been bred to the previous year (and the year before that), what her calf looked like, and how her calves might be improved.

Scotty supervised the installation of our truck scale. Our bull calves were weighed at intervals and the weight recorded to indicate the rate of their growth. Scotty conducted a controlled breeding program. He picked a specific bull from the lot in front of the house to breed to each cow when she was ready, bringing the bull away when service was complete. He would make twenty to thirty trips each day from 5:30 A.M. (when he arrived on his cow pony, Granny) to 6:00 P.M., when he left for his home two miles west of us. In this way, over the years most of the "linebacks," "sore eyes," and "peaked-ass" calves were bred out of the herd. What we had left were big for their age and very uniform. By the mid-1930s the Carpenter Hereford herd was the seventh largest in the United States. We grazed over sixteen thousand acres of fenced pasture, put up fifteen hundred tons of hay, and cut nearly six hundred acres of grain every year.

My lifelong interest in the breeding of cattle was deepened immeasurably by working with Scotty Annand, who taught me patience. It takes years, for example, to get a breeding program timed properly so that the calves are arriving within a short period of time and the mothers are with them when the breeding period starts again.

All the while, the ranch also had the benefit of Evan Marr's management skill—derived from his Vermont Yankee upbringing—and a banker's eye on the dollar, ensuring better-than-usual control over employees, purchasing, and all-around efficiency. I took as much time as I could from my law practice to help Evan with the selling. We sold to anybody and everybody—the Ute Indians, the Mormons, the outlaws, even some sheepmen—and we sold by telegraph, by sample steaks, and by hospitality (bull buyers always got the guest room and a meal). We sold to Jim Black from the New Mexico and Arizona ranches of the Victoria Land and Cattle Company, who bought five carloads of bull calves every year for nearly ten years because he could count on an extra 50 pounds of meat on a 1,500-pound steer from a Carpenter bull. In addition, Jim got a bargain at $100 per head for nine-month-old calves weighing from 450 to 500 pounds. And all our buyers knew that we stood behind our cattle, making good on every animal that failed in any way.

As we moved into the 1930s and 1940s, beef marketing procedures kept changing. In 1927, the Grading Service of the United States Department of Agriculture began grading beef carcasses for *quality* and stamping the grade on the outside of the carcass. In addition to differences in quality there were differences in the *quantity* of edible meat in a carcass. This created a demand by consumers that a designation of both quantity *and* quality be stamped on a carcass. I was an energetic advocate of this dual grading idea, but it was opposed bitterly by the meat packers, who helped to delay its implementation for many years.

Meanwhile, during the lean years of the depression I became acutely aware that one of our largest expenses was the cost of registering our purebred calves in the Herd Book of the American Hereford Association. The cost of pedigree papers rose from twenty-five cents to a dollar per head and the initiation fee from twenty-five to fifty dollars. These increases were made while the association's annual reports showed big profits and the membership was doubled. Surplus funds were used to give generous prize money to a small coterie of breeders who were on the board of directors of the association.

One year, when the association failed to make public its annual audit, a number of western breeders, including myself, decided to investigate the situation. I was selected for the job and went to the association's plush offices in Kansas City. I found that the association was run by an oligarchy of a few men. The directors were elected at the annual meeting in Kansas City, and as no voting proxies were allowed, a small clique of local members were able to keep their own choices in office.

The boss of this oligarchy was R. J. Kinzer, the perennial secre-tary and treasurer. With the aim of interesting wealthy people in Hereford purebred cattle, he had put several of them on the board of directors. One of his choices was Harvey Firestone, the Detroit rubber baron, who knew less about cattle than I knew about the sport of curling.

I further found that many thousands of dollars in prizes at the big stock shows went to these wealthy directors of the American Hereford Association. Since the judges at the Hereford part of the shows were selected and paid for by the association with money that we ordinary members paid to get pedigree papers for our cattle, they were able to dictate the kind of outside conforma-tion that they considered to be the ideal animal in the future. It was partly their show-ring judgment during the 1940s that led some breeders to take up the "comprest" fad of producing smaller bulls to meet the alleged demand of consumers for smaller beef cuts. Unfortunately, "comprest" breeding led to dwarfism in a Hereford herd, which could only be cured by selling the entire herd and returning to traditional breeding prin-ciples.

When I made my report on all these matters, it caused a rebel-lion among Hereford members who did not belong to the clique whose cattle seemed to be favored with prizes at the stock shows. The upshot was the creation of Performance Registry In-ternational. It proposed a revolution in the search for superior sires based not on pedigrees but on scientific tests of an animal's quality. Performance Registry was made up at first largely of Texas and Oklahoma breeders who made performance tests to guide them in their selection of breeding stock. These tests con-sisted of weighing calves at a known age and by dividing their weight by the number of days of age to get a figure representing the animal's ability to convert feed into beef. It was, in short, a long-overdue scientific method, replacing the visual inspections of the stock show judges.

Performance Registry International caught on quickly in the years after that first meeting. It struck me from the start as a benchmark in the history of beef cattle improvement. I hastened to join it as a founding director, and throughout the 1950s I en-joyed traveling about the country promoting it. I served without pay as its treasurer for some years and then as president. During my tenure I hired Dale Lynch, a recent graduate of Montana

State University, as its full-time secretary with an office in Denver.

The new group attracted livestock members from all forty-eight states and from many Canadian provinces and foreign countries. It elevated cattle raising out of its narrow orbit of a few breeds into the larger world of modern technology by establishing standards of excellence based on the day-by-day growth rate of young cattle. By using computerized progeny records, it created a common language for sellers and buyers of cattle, which increased the market for progressive producers.

The registry issued papers of superior worth to crossbred animals which met specifications drawn from their growth records. Since crossbreeds could not be registered with the purebred associations, this chance to get papers caused great expansion of the practice of crossbreeding. Through the decades into the 1960s, cattlemen took up crossbreeding in a big way—Herefords and Shorthorns and Angus and then, by importation, Brahmas, Charolais, Limousin, and Simmental from France, Romaldo from Italy, Black Friesian from Germany, and the rest of the European strains noted for bone and muscle development. Because of the commercial success of these crosses, cattlemen everywhere came to realize that the points of difference between the various breeds were extremely superficial. As things turned out, the breed associations found that their prestige was enhanced when they began applying the computerized methods of Performance Registry International to their own system of issuing papers for their purebreds.

"Do You Want to Hear a Story?"

Editor's Note: It is fitting that the final chapter of Farrington Carpenter's autobiography be written by his eldest son, Edward F. Carpenter, who was with his father during the last weeks of his life.

I suppose as our father moved through his seventies that he slowed up a bit. If so, none of his children—Rosamond, Willis, or I—noticed it. From 1956 on he called his ranch "Carpenter and Williams Meat Type Herefords." Evan Marr had left to go into the military construction business. George ("Scotty") Annand had bought a ranch for his own purebred herd of Herefords. Melvin Williams, the son of his neighbor, Max Williams, took charge of his cattle, keeping weight records for Performance Registry and the usual pedigree data of the herd for the American Hereford Association. Dad made the rounds of the ranch almost daily in his four-wheel-drive Bronco in any kind of weather to see how his Herefords were doing. The ungallant Bronco dumped him into a ditch in 1975 and then rolled backwards over him, forcing him to limp home, none the worse for wear. And he was ready at the drop of a hat to shove off anywhere to give a talk—to livestock men, lawyers, politicians, Princeton or Harvard alumni, anyone who invited him to speak on any subject. People who had heard his stories over and over seemed always glad to hear them again.

Soon after his eightieth birthday Dad announced that he had organized a new group, Better Beef, Inc., to replace what he re-

TOP: *Ferry and Eunice, about 1950.*
BOTTOM: *Ferry and Rosamond, about 1966.*

garded as the prevailing outmoded beef marketing system. Better Beef proposed to merchandise cattle along principles used by supermarkets in selling soap. When a reporter asked him if he ever regretted the time that he had spent raising cattle, he replied: "There's not much money in it, son. And I never found it anything but a pain in the neck some of the time. But hold on! It was the good life for me and my family—the freedom of it, the joy of being able to tell the rest of the world to go to hell any time I felt like it, which was often."

He was saddened in 1974 when his second wife, Rosamond Underwood Carpenter, died. He wrote and published in her memory a handsome illustrated booklet recounting in detail the story of how she had come from Smith College with Dorothy Woodruff in 1916 as the first teachers at Elkhead School in the wilds near his Oak Point homestead. Writing the booklet seemed to stimulate his old resolve to write his autobiography. As he approached his ninetieth year he spent more and more time in his big library gathering research materials for his book. He put it together slowly, with much rewriting to get his chapters the way he thought that they should be.

Meanwhile, the annual fall sale of weaner calves on the first Saturday of October handily outclassed Christmas and the Fourth of July as red-letter days for the family and the families employed at the Carpenter-Williams Ranch. Though Dad's handwriting was becoming nearly illegible, he prepared for the sale by writing personal letters to many of his old customers and making tapes for his radio advertising. Even at ninety he retained the clear, strong voice of the true pitchman, and he never lost his enthusiasm for his product. He was a superb salesman.

In fact, that clear, strong voice of his that had served him so well as cowboy and lawyer caused him to be cast in the role of a TV star for his old friend Charlotte Perry. Charlotte had cofounded with Portia Mansfield the Perry-Mansfield School at Strawberry Park near Steamboat Springs. Through the years, their school had trained such famous dancers as Hanya Holm, Agnes de Mille, and Merce Cunningham. The actor Dustin Hoffman had studied theater at Strawberry Park. When Portia Mansfield died in January 1979, Charlotte produced in her memory a thirty-minute film, "Divine Madness." Its world premiere occurred in Denver on June 22, 1979, with Dad serving as a narrator. Later it was shown as a TV documentary throughout the United States.

And finally came the date, August 10, 1980, which was Dad's birthday. It was impossible for Rosamond and Willis and I, who were with him at the ranch celebration that day, to believe it. But there it was—our father's ninety-fourth birthday. He was growing noticeably older and slower in his physical abilities, and all three of us wondered if he could make it through one more northwestern Colorado winter. And yet his talk—cheerful and as entertaining as ever—belied any apprehension on his part that he might be approaching his end.

He followed the construction of our new irrigation system with special concern over the cost, asking if the final figure would exceed the $100,000 limit we had placed on this project. Although few ranchers would have undertaken such a project at ninety-four, he did not hesitate because he always looked to the future of the ranch. Placing 210 additional acres under irrigation would make it possible to raise enough hay and pasture so that the herd could be substantially increased.

This project, of course, was directly related to his next main interest, the 1980 fall bull sale. The Carpenter-Williams Ranch sale on October 4, 1980, drew the biggest crowd we ever had, from fifteen states on a beautiful golden fall day. From the tall cottonwoods along the Yampa to the clouds drifting over the Flat Tops to the south, it was a day for confidence and hope and hard work, culminating a year's effort. As usual on sale day, Dad crawled into the bed of the pickup unassisted and rang the old Dawson cowbell to start the sale. He regaled the big crowd with a couple of old cowboy stories and explained how the sale would be conducted. It was not a disappointment. The top calf was a 3.41-pound-per-day gainer. While the average was lower than the previous year because of low cattle prices generally, and drought conditions in many places, not a bull calf remained unsold at the close of the day.

After the sale, Dad held court for another half hour before we could persuade him to return to the living room and his chair by the fireplace. But by the time he got to the house he admitted that he was all tuckered out, took off his boots for a nap, and we saw him next at breakfast on Sunday. The sale had been a glorious day for him and he rose to the occasion, but he slept nearly twenty of each twenty-four hours for the next two weeks.

Not long after the sale, Dad received a letter from the American Hereford Association inviting him to be present in Kansas City on November 10, 1980, for his induction to the Gallery of Honor of the Hereford Heritage Hall of the Assocation. The gallery was established in 1978 and constituted the Hereford industry's Hall of Fame. The association's citation for the award read:

> This early day law school graduate has carved a successful career in law and the registered Hereford business and continues as an active Hereford rancher at the age of 94. He has been a champion of the cause of performance testing for more than 40 years and at one time was labelled in the livestock press as the "nation's top salesman" for performance programs. The Carpenter registered Hereford herd traces to 25 foundation cows purchased in 1909.

Without saying "I told you so," Dad could not disguise the pleasure that this recognition by his fellow purebred breeders gave him. We knew better than to try to persuade him not to make the effort to get to Kansas City. He spent nearly two weeks resting to charge his battery for the trip. When we met him at the Denver airport to take the plane to Kansas City, the old blue eyes sparkled and his pleasure was evident. Word was out that he was coming and again he held court in the lobby of the Muhlebach Hotel and the AHA building until the appointed hour. He was the last of the six honorees to be called. I just knew he would tell a story to the crowd. But he smiled broadly, held up the medal for all to see, and sat down. The applause was prolonged.

The flight home was quiet. He was very weary and slept much of the time after our return to the ranch. He suffered a small stroke the Sunday after Thanksgiving Day. Viola Henderson and Mel Williams took him to the hospital despite his objections. Doctor Monahan took some tests on Monday and said that he could go home. Dad weakened rapidly after his return, but he was content to be at home.

The last few days he was nearly comatose. But the day before he died, he gathered up the last of his reserve strength and raised his head. Vi Henderson supported him as he looked her square in the eye with the famous twinkle and said, "Do you want to hear a story?" Then he settled back and never spoke again.

That should be his epitaph. I am convinced that he planned it as his final phrase. He died quietly about 6:30 P.M. on Friday, December 12, 1980.

The memorial service for Dad was held in the Hayden Congregational Church on December 20, 1980. It consisted of five vignettes of his past recalled by five dear friends. Becky Love told of his law practice; Bobby Robinson recalled early Elkhead and Hayden days; Tom Lasater detailed his pioneering in the livestock industry; Marvin Klemme told of his years with the Grazing Service; and Bill Gossard summed up his career as raconteur, politician, legislator, benefactor, and inspiration to all who knew him.

On January 30, 1981, a house-senate joint resolution by the Fifty-third General Assembly of the Colorado State Legislature memorialized his career. It featured a moving tribute by former Governor John Love. Passage of the resolution evoked a standing ovation.

INDEX